FRIENDS OF ACPL

Stranger
in the Pines

Stranger in the Pines

By MAY McNEER

Illustrated by Lynd Ward

Houghton Mifflin Company Boston

Books by
MAY McNEER

America's Abraham Lincoln
America's Mark Twain
Little Baptiste
My Friend Mac

ALLEN COUNTY PUBLIC LIBRARY
FORT WAYNE, INDIANA

COPYRIGHT © 1971 BY MAY MCNEER WARD
ALL RIGHTS RESERVED. NO PART OF THIS WORK MAY BE
REPRODUCED OR TRANSMITTED IN ANY FORM BY ANY MEANS,
ELECTRONIC OR MECHANICAL, INCLUDING PHOTOCOPYING AND
RECORDING, OR BY ANY INFORMATION STORAGE OR RETRIEVAL
SYSTEM, WITHOUT PERMISSION IN WRITING FROM THE PUBLISHER.
LIBRARY OF CONGRESS CATALOG CARD NUMBER 74-142826
ISBN 0-395-12367-4
PRINTED IN THE U.S.A.
Second Printing c

7021585

To our grandsons,
Alex Weedon Haynes and
Mark McNeer Savage

Stranger in the Pines

Chapter 1

A<small>DAM</small> <small>RAN</small> for the river. Now and again he slowed his long legs to look fearfully over his shoulder. He saw a man glancing at him and he ran again, leaping over refuse in an alley as he dodged through, bumping passers-by on the street, which sent him faster toward the fish and salt scent of the Delaware River.

It was scarcely daylight on this spring morning, and the sun was a pale rosy glow behind the fleeing boy and the sprawling city. Yet wharves were already alive with seamen loading tall-masted vessels, and people still surly from crawling out of warm quilts were thronging Front Street. Adam came to a sudden halt. Panting, eyes darting about at workmen and sailors, he could see no one who appeared to be interested in him. He shifted the worn leather knapsack a little on his shoulder. Philadelphia and the road out of it toward the western wilderness lay behind him. He had chosen not to run that way, for that was where they would look for him. Now he must get across the river quickly.

How was he to do it? He had no money to pay his fare on the new steam ferry chugging its magical way over, nor even on one of the large rowboats constantly crossing to the New Jersey shore and back. Was that fellow staring at him? Adam dodged behind a stack of bales and peered around it.

He sighed in relief. The man was strolling away. Adam stared desperately at the water. Could he find a berth as cabin boy on one of those clipper ships and disappear forever from this city? He set his jaws until his teeth ached, knowing that he could not even ask on one of those ships.

A teamster standing beside his rig was talking to a flatboatman: "I can't wait longer. You get me a-going to Jersey or I'll find another boat."

The boatman growled, "How can I pull two sweeps? That no-account varmint of a rower, damn his eyes, he's in some grog shop already, or sleeping off last night."

The teamster reached for his horses' bridles and turned away. Seeing this the boatman glared at the crowd, his eyes searching for his absent man. He saw Adam.

Adam drew back a little, knowing that his clothing told everybody that he was apprenticed to a blacksmith and ironworker. He had forgotten to remove his soiled leather apron. He untied and dropped it, kicking it behind the bales. Then he stepped out and approached the boatman.

"Sir — sir, I can pull a sweep." His voice rang out

louder than he had intended, and he lowered it. "Will you take me on?"

The man scowled, looking him over, then bawled after his departing fare, "Here! I can take you over. Wait!"

To Adam he said, "Well, you look strong enough to do it. Apprentice, ain't you? Can you make a crossing and back before your master expects you? It will be a good half hour or more."

"Aye, sir." Adam jumped to the flatboat and took a hand in getting the team aboard and the big wagon safely blocked. He felt sick in the pit of his stomach as he tried not to think of his master. The owner of the flatboat took the other sweep, and the teamster lit his pipe as he steadied his animals on the swaying platform. Adam shrugged his British campaign knapsack off and dropped it near as he grasped the long oar. He soon caught the rhythm of the sweeps, and with each strong pull the city was farther behind him and his fear a little easier. Sun up, the river was active with moving craft, with shouts and calls of boatmen echoing over the water. On an upsweep Adam lifted his eyes to see the large brick building which dominated the waterfront. THE JERVIS SHIPPING COMPANY was painted in black letters across it. One need not know how to read to recognize it. Memory of a thin old man all in black, pounding a silver-topped cane on the scarred wooden floor of his counting house office, brought such a wave of fury that Adam had to swallow hard as he worked and blinked sweat from his eyes.

At Cooper's Landing, or Camden as it was now called, on the Jersey shore, the flatboat came to its usual place below town and pulled in to the bank. Adam thrust his knapsack over his arm and sprang forward to help his employer lay the planks to shore, then waited to guide the horses over. He glanced at the grassy riverbank, then at the big flatboatman returning to his craft, scarcely hearing a shout to come aboard and take a hand with the new fare now creaking forward. Adam took a deep breath, realizing that he had made a kind of promise to pull the sweep back to the city, and the flatboatman had to have a man for the off oar.

"Take a hand with that fare," roared the boat owner. "Get that front wheel chocked!"

Adam whirled about and ran. The wagoner shouted, and the boatman howled a string of oaths that should have set Adam's ears afire. Small boys playing in the dusty road took after him yelling, "Stop thief!" as boys always did at anybody who ran. Adam outdistanced them easily, cut in behind a tangle of outbuildings, and did not stop until he had left Camden town behind him. He came on a long, sandy road stretching into a forest. Wagons and carriages were moving along it from the ferry landings. Nobody glanced his way as Adam set out with dust from their wheels settling down on him. Others on foot caught up and passed him without a look, all in a hurry to get home.

As the day advanced his stomach protested at its emptiness, and yet he did not pause to rest or try to fill it. In the warm springtime sun he moved doggedly on past farmhouses where barking dogs discouraged him from asking for work and a meal. As farms grew fewer and thickets of laurel, holly, and tangled vines more frequent, the sun went down in a blaze of color behind pine trees with wind whispering in their tops. He was far from the city, and he was now in country entirely strange. Philadelphia was the only place he could remember since his birth there in 1815. It was the center of his world, and it had been the only place he could call home. Never before had he ventured outside those streets, for since he was seven years old he had worked for Bolt Sherman, blacksmith and ironworker. As he thought of his master, dizziness made him sway, and again he felt a sickness nearly overcome him.

He stumbled into the woods and dropped down on chilly earth behind the shelter of a holly bush, covering his face with his hands as he remembered the terrible thing he had done. When the moon rose he was drained of all feeling but complete weariness, and he fell asleep with his head resting on his father's old knapsack.

Chapter 2

W<small>HEN HE WOKE</small> he first thought he had been sleeping in Waterworks Park. Eyes still closed, he listened for sounds of the city. Clang of horseshoe striking cobbles, creak of wagon, noise of voices in a chorus of shouts and street cries were morning sounds so familiar that his stomach tightened when he realized they were not there. Where was he? Memory came suddenly. He was lying under a holly bush. Who knew where? As he crawled out and lifted his face to the sun, he drew a breath of relief, for he had escaped his enemies, at least for now, and he was on his way. He opened wide his eyes, his mouth, and his nostrils to drink in the strange scent of freedom. The road before him was empty of life, and Adam claimed it as his own.

Where would it lead him? For some years he had

worked and lived in his master's house with people he disliked, and always he had worked toward and believed in his father's return. Now he was alone and his only companion was a raging determination to go northward to some city, probably New York, lose himself in the crowd, and somehow educate himself. His hands closed into fists as he told himself that he would never be found and brought back to Philadelphia, and that he would return of his own free will someday to clear himself and to seek his revenge. How he could do this he did not know, nor how long it would take. He was penniless and must find work first — and soon.

After a while thirst dried his mouth, so he welcomed sight of a run sparkling over the roots of cedars, and knelt to drink. At first he drew back because of the dark color of this water, like strong tea. Then he cupped it in his hands, to find it cold and with a taste of iron. As he plodded along the road again his stomach grumbled so loudly that at last he could think of nothing but food.

He sat down on a tuft of grass beside the road wondering if being free meant that eventually he would starve to death, and if that eventuality was soon to be with him. He was a city lad accustomed to a household that was never niggardly with food. On his master's table there would be a hearty breakfast of porridge, milk, bread, and molasses. At this thought Adam closed his eyes, clamped his jaws together, and clutched his belt. He did not really notice the sound of creaking wheels and the approaching clop of a horse's hoofs.

"Ho, me lad, are you turned to a pillar of salt like the misfortunate wife of old Lot? What ails you? A pain in the gut?"

Adam popped his eyes open and let his arms drop. He found himself staring at a sheet-topped Jersey wagon, a mare with a knowing look in her off eye, and a man lounging easily on the seat. He fixed his astonished gaze on the man. In the city Adam had rubbed elbows with people of many lands, and yet not one like this stranger. He saw a parted wave of white hair beneath the jaunty hat and an equally white tuft on the chin. Green eyes straddled a long nose.

"Lad, be you taken with a wonderful zickness?"

With that the fellow jumped down from his wagon. "Hurt, does it? Ain't right still? It kreissels you, me lad?"

Adam straightened up. "I'm all right, sir. I'm not sickened."

The stranger clasped his hands behind his back and teetered on his heels and toes. "Well, then, why for do you sit like that? Are you starving?"

Receiving a nod the stranger stepped to the back of his wagon, climbed over the tailgate, and emerged with a bottle of ale under one arm, a sack of apples under the other, in one hand a loaf, and in the other a wedge of farmer's cheese of the kind Adam had often seen on stalls at the German end of the market. He tried not to wolf down the food like a wild beast, and yet most of it disappeared that way. The man went to tie a bag of oats under the horse's long lip. Filled with bread, cheese, and ale, Adam raised his eye as he bit into an apple.

He saw trousers of dun-colored broadcloth with straps under the boots, a flowered waistcoat, green flowing cravat, and a long-tailed coat. The shirt was scarcely visible, and just as well, too, for it was none too clean. A tiny ink horn, stoppered with a cork, was pinned to the

lapel of the coat, and a goose quill was thrust through the band of his hat. This must be a traveling scribe who made his living writing letters and documents for unlettered folk.

"Now that the inner man is satisfied, I introduce myself mit you. Rembrandt Kip. Who are you?" He thrust out his hand.

"Adam Quinn," taking the hand with a shake.

"Whither bound, me lad? If in the forward direction, toward Long-a-Coming and Bogquake, why not join me in the wagon?"

Adam nodded, saying, "Mr. Kip, I am beholden to you. Never did anything taste so good as this meal. I will ride along with you, and gladly."

"Good! Then come aboard."

He removed the oat bag from the horse's licking tongue, looked inside, found it empty, patted the animal on its long, lugubrious nose, and jumped to the seat, picking up the reins as he landed. Adam stepped up to swing his legs in beside the driver. As they jogged along there was no absence of conversation, although for some miles the talk came mainly from Rembrandt Kip.

"You wonder who I am, don't you? You wonder why I talk like this in a fascinating mixture of local speech, don't you, lad? You are tongue-tied at the apparition of this human distilfink from the Pennsylvania Dutch country? And well may you be. I have long traveled the roads of Pennsylvania and New Jersey, and I have learned the speech habits of them all — the Dutchman as well as the piney with his Jersey downtown gab. So you wonder why I mix my gabbing, do you?"

He paused, so Adam said rather hesitantly, "Well, sir,

maybe I do wonder a little. I never before heard a man talk like you."

"Happily I'll tell you. But don't you give me away, laddie. I fit my speech to my customers, whenever I can manage it. Do you believe Rembrandt Kip to be my name?"

"I — well — I — aye, sir."

Adam was alarmed, thinking perhaps he had taken up with a madman or a wild showman of some sort.

"I'll tell you then. I am no more a Dutchman than you be, even in name. French by birth, although living in Hanover, Pennsylvania, since tender infancy. My real name is Hyacinthe Lafitte. Believe it or not, and it's easier not, that was the name on my baptismal paper, placed there by a priest in France. Now, I ask of you, can I paint the solemn faces of German farmers and their plump Fraus in Sunday best when I bear the name of Hyacinthe Lafitte? Or of plain folk in Quaker gray and pious thoughts? No. I would not have the gall to ask them to let me. So, for the sake of my honorable profession, I changed my name so long ago that not even the good folk of Hanover can remember the real one."

Adam stole a glance at him. "You said you paint farmers and their wives. Is that your trade?"

"Yes, me lad, it is. I started out as an apprentice." Here he shot a shrewd look at his companion, taking in the style of nankeen breeches, osnaburg shirt, and leather jerkin. "Um — to Master Samuel Enredi Stetinious in the printing trade. When I finished my bound-out years with him he took me on as a journeyman printer. After some years of settled life the work palled on me. I developed an itch to go the road up, as they say in Pennsylvania back country.

If need forces me I can stop in a town on me travels and do a job for a printer, but that I never do so long as I can ramble the roads and paint. I travel the Pennsylvania highways and byways in autumn, work in the Hanover printshop in winter, and spring finds me setting out down Jersey — as you see me doing."

"How did you learn to paint pictures?"

"Ah, Master Stetinious was a limner of no mean order himself. I learned from him. He was no vagabond neither, as I am, and he had a finer talent, too. That I know well. Yet I think I leave farmers and their wives and children happier for a picture or two hanging in their parlors. I stay out of cities where the physiognomists take coppers for nonsensical portraits in the marketplaces. They call their monstrosities art! Have you seen how they do by laying a face against a sheet of paper?"

"Aye, sir," said Adam, laughing. "I have watched that device trace a head on paper to please a servant girl. I thought it funny."

"Funny it is, indeed. And they call that a portrait. The silhouettist with his black paper and shears is far better than that. Yet nothing to compare with a painted likeness."

"Do you leave your wife while you travel, Mr. Kip?"

The painter flapped the reins and tried in vain to hurry up his horse. "I have no Frau. Once I had, and for ten years. Her name was Wilhelmina, and a hearty, springy lass she was, too. She ran away with a devil-may-care keelboatman and vanished up the Allegheny River."

"Why didn't you catch them up and take her home?"

Kip made a comic face. "Had you seen the fellow you would not ask. He had fists like hams and was known to be an eye gouger and a stomper. Not I! I don't forget my

Wilhelmina — but that was a long time ago. Many a girl I know in many a town, but none have I found that I want to marry who might want to marry me. Adam, do you like the girls?"

Adam turned fiery red and pulled on his red hair. Kip asked, "How old are you?"

"Fifteen." He was sullen, resenting the amusement in his companion's eyes.

"You're scared silly of the swish of a petticoat. Hummmm! Well, time enough for the girls when you settle, I warrant."

The slow horse plodded on, never passing another vehicle, although some passed it. The countryside was heavily wooded with now and then a small brown stream to cross by wooden bridge, and if there was no bridge the old mare walked sedately through the water, pulling the wagon along after her. At dusk Mr. Kip reined in his horse.

"Whoa, there, Hendrickje! Whoa, I say."

So saying he leaped over the wheel into the road. Adam supposed that Mr. Kip was an old man, for his hair was white, and yet this limner was as nimble as a ropewalker in a raree show.

"We are on a turnoff road to Long-a-Coming and will get there in the end, but not so directly. I have a customer beyond, out on the road to Bogquake, and it is my custom to stay with those good farming people the night. Ah — how that Mercy Willowby can cook! I dream of her apple dumplings when I am sitting by my lonely campfire eating fried fatback and johnnycake."

He busied himself making a fire and Adam went to gather sticks to keep it burning, then he filled a pot with

13

water from the gurgling run nearby. A warm and comforting ease settled on him as he stretched out on the grass after supper and listened to Mr. Kip. And as he listened he clasped his hands behind his neck and stared sleepily up into the spreading branches of a buttonwood tree. He scarcely listened when Kip paused.

"You are a runaway bound boy, aren't you, Adam?"

As if a shot had zinged at him Adam leaped to his feet and took off into the woods. He tripped over a root and went sprawling. Kip guffawed, sitting up to slap his knee.

"Come back, Adam Quinn! Rembrandt Kip has never yet turned in man or boy, and never will. Secrets are safe with me, laddie, and many have I gathered in, too. Come now — sit you down and tell me about it."

Adam, furious with himself for such a retreat, returned slowly and dropped down beside the fire. Hunching over, he turned his face aside as he said, "I'm a runaway bound boy, Mr. Kip. I won't go back. I can't — I — I —"

His voice died out in a painful silence, and then Rembrandt Kip said slowly, "Ah, I see. Ja, ja, oui, and yes, indeed. I understand."

A misery settled in Adam's insides, for he knew that Kip did not understand. He didn't know the terrible thing that Adam could not tell anyone. As the moon climbed over pine tops, Kip crawled into his wagon, where he kept a space just large enough to accommodate his body among frames, canvases, and brushes, and slept amid pungent odors of turpentine and paints. He tossed out a rough blanket to Adam, who rolled himself in it beside the dying fire.

Chapter 3

THEY CAME into the little village of Long-a-Coming with Rembrandt Kip waving to everybody in sight and greeted by everyone with a "Hallo, limner" and "How be you, Kip?"

They pulled up before the Stagecoach Inn, where Kip invited Adam to come in and have a mug of ale. Adam shook his head and offered to stay with the wagon, for he was not anxious to show himself in a taproom where the stage from Camden stopped on its way to Clamtown on the coast. Kip shrugged and disappeared just as the coach came rattling into Long-a-Coming, drawing up with a flourish behind old Hendrickje and her sheet wagon. Adam jerked around to watch the passengers as they got down. He was relieved to see nobody who looked like pursuit to him.

Then a man jumped to the road from beside the driver. Adam fixed his eyes on him. He was a strong-looking fellow in seaman's clothing and agile for a man with gray hair. He stood a moment with eyes moving slowly about the street. They met Adam's. This chap had odd eyes, with one lid wide open and the other a slit. Adam shivered and drew back into the wagon, fingers clutching palms. He heard a sound of slow footsteps, the creaking of a door, and gathered courage to look again. The man's back was disappearing into the taproom. A huge sigh escaped Adam. Slowly he straightened his fingers, and yet he was still stiff and withdrawn when Kip returned.

As they drove away Kip glanced at his companion and said, "Bound boys run away every day, Adam. You better wipe that startled-buck look from your face or somebody will catch you sure enough."

Adam settled down with a sheepish grin, growing easier as the day advanced; and once as they jogged along he surprised himself by softly whistling an Irish tune remembered from his father long ago. Then, with that memory, he fell silent again, thoughts drifting painfully into the bitter question that had been with him so long. Why had Patrick Quinn never written to his son, although he had promised him faithfully? Why?

Although the sun was still above the pines it was growing dark in clumps of cedars and in rusty swamp waters. Without looking he recognized cedar bogs now, for the thickly entwined branches of those trees sawed against each other to make a sound like the devil's own fiddle as a wind came up to set them swaying. Mr. Kip was quiet, head nodding over his reins. Uneasiness crept into Adam's spirit from the darkness and the moaning in the bogs. He tried to stop himself from wondering why the eyes of that seaman made him so uncomfortable.

"I'm turning fancies in my mind," he told himself. "He wasn't searching for me."

Just the same he ducked his head aside when the stagecoach passed them in a cloud of dust, even as he tried to believe that the man was just a sailor on his way to join the crew of a ship docked at one of the Jersey coastal towns.

Kip shook himself awake and began to ramble on, telling of his own life, of places where he had been, of things he had seen. His eyes lit up when he spoke of painting.

"Ah, Adam, I wish I might have been a man of talent. I am not. I can please wives and goodmen of farms and villages. Yet I am no competition to artists in the cities. Have you ever heard of Rembrandt van Rijn? No? Well — there was the greatest artist of all time. Though he died long years ago in the Netherlands, I have not yet seen his masterworks. Only heard of them, and seen copies."

"Is that important to you, Mr. Kip?" wondered Adam, never having heard anyone speak of pictures in that way.

"That it is. Aye. Ja, indeed. It kreissels me much not to have seen those paintings. And I tell you, Adam, my dream is to put by enough pounds and pence to take me across the seas to Amsterdam to see them. Rembrandt cared nothing for the rich burghers whose portraits he painted. That he did only for bread and a roof over his head. He lived among the poor and painted them by choice." Kip clucked to his horse and said, "I'll get over there sometime."

Adam thought of his own uncertain future, and little enough it seemed. Yet he knew that neither Kip nor any man had as much determination as he did. He could do what he willed himself to do. That, also, he believed. And he was beginning to know vaguely what he would do someday.

"And now, Adam Quinn, what do you mean to do with yourself?"

Adam jerked as though struck, and moved as if about to leap out. Was this man able to see into his head? Kip held him firmly by an arm, laughing, "Now, lad, don't be so afrighted. Anybody would think you had killed someone."

At this Adam gave a lunge out of Kip's grasp and jumped to the road, where he fell in the dust. Hendrickje stopped. Kip was beside him before he could regain his feet, holding his shoulders in a tight grip.

"You won't get up until you listen to me, Adam Quinn! I told you I will not turn you in, and I don't want to know what you have done. Now, get back in the wagon, you daft creature."

On their way once more, with Adam silently brushing dust from his clothing, Kip said, "I was only asking you where you are going and what you mean to do for work?"

"My trade is iron. First, I must get a job."

"You can do blacksmithing?"

"Aye."

"Then Bogquake is the place for you. That's a furnace town where bog iron is cooked and molded. Mr. Edwards is the ironmaster. There is also a smithy, and down Jersey they aren't too careful about asking for a man's work papers. Mayhap you can get work there.

"Stop with me tonight at the Willowby farm, which lies halfway to the town anyway. A bright young miss has persuaded her father to have his likeness limned by me — or so I think. They expect me about this time of the month and will give you welcome for the night. Since tomorrow is the Sabbath they can drive you to Bogquake, thus saving shoe leather for you."

Approaching the farm toward the end of the day the old mare's pace slowed to a walk that was scarcely motion, and Adam and Kip were silent. Suddenly Adam spoke, "Mr. Kip, I've been thinking — I — these people are expecting you, not me. I don't want to come in on strangers like that."

"Now, me lad, don't talk silly. The Willowbys will absolutely insist on it. After all, Friends do welcome strangers."

"Friends? Friends of yours, Mr. Kip. Not my friends."

"I meant Quakers. All Quakers hereabouts are hospitable, you know, why once —"

Adam reached for his knapsack, saying grimly, "Then stop here. I will not go to any house of Quakers."

Kip drew in the horse and turned to stare at his companion, frowning, "And now may I ask what is wrong with Quakers?"

Adam's face was hard as he said, "I owe you for your kindness, but I will not consort with Quakers. Do you want to know why I was bound out at seven years old? Why I am hunted and hounded? Who did this to me?" His voice was loud and yet he had to stop a moment to halt a sudden trembling.

"My father left me with my grandfather after my mother died. My grandfather made me set my mark on those apprentice papers when I could not write my name. My grandfather is a Quaker!"

"Your father — was he of Friends Meeting, too?"

"No, that he was not. He was Irish and a Roman Catholic, though not much of a churchgoing man. He was a soldier in the British Army, one who stayed here when his service was out. My mother married him against her father's orders."

Kip looked skeptical. "Ah, then why did he leave you with your Quaker grandfather?"

Adam suddenly was without anger, and he felt a great weariness. His tone was low and sad, "He went into the western wilderness to make a place for himself. He said he would come back for me in a short while. My grandfather agreed to look out for me until then, since I was given his name. But he hated me as he hated my father. He wanted only to be rid of me." Adam burst out, "You don't believe me, do you?"

"Aye, lad, I do, but did your father not write to you?"

Adam's face seemed to close in with his unhappiness, so Kip said hastily, "Mayhap he did and they were lost on the way."

After a time, when only the slow sound of the horse's hoofs punctuated a silence, Kip asked, "Why do you run from your master now? And after all those years?"

"I'll say no more." Adam jumped from the wagon and reached for his knapsack, slinging it about his arms as he turned. "Thankee, Mr. Kip, and farewell."

"Hey, laddie!" shouted Kip as he reined in Hendrickje, "Wait — hold on —"

Adam was already moving along on the dusty road toward the east, where a rosy afterglow was fading behind a gathering of clouds. At that moment a small whirlwind burst from behind the barn and came at them. Adam

halted in his tracks. He saw a gray dress and a pair of stockings flashing by in a cloud of dust, with a long braid whipping about and arms reaching for a squealing pig.

"Come here!"

The girl threw herself at the animal, missed, and landed face down in the dirt. The pig made straight for Adam, who had more than once chased pigs in city streets for sport. He reached out and closed in on the animal, holding on tightly to the right front leg and the left hind foot, and so managing to thrust the pig under one arm. When he could look he saw the girl on her feet, and heard Kip laughing uproariously in the wagon. A man and a woman were advancing rapidly from the farmyard. The tight-lipped woman said, "Tranquility, does thee think thyself a hoyden?"

The burly man pushed his oddly shaped leather hat backward on his head until the neck protector flap lay on his shoulders. With a twinkle in his eye he said, "Daughter, thee has scandalized thy mother. At ease. Reinforcements have arrived. The enemy has surrendered."

The girl, suddenly aware of this strange young fellow, blushed hotly and rubbed her cheeks, smearing dust in a wide swath across her face. She hastily smoothed down her long skirt, adjusted her collar, and glared at Adam.

Mrs. Willowby said severely, "Tranquility, go to thy room at once and pray for a spirit of quiet and contemplation to cleanse thyself of disorderliness."

" 'Twould be better, Mercy, if she made use of soft soap and water. She looks like a campground after a late bivouac."

At this Kip laughed again and then, assuming a sober

face, he addressed himself to the stiff Mrs. Willowby. "This is Adam Quinn. He traveled with me from near Camden and is going on to Bogquake."

Mrs. Willowby made no reply, but her husband said heartily, "Then the least we can do, Adam Quinn, in return for ambushing the enemy, is to offer thee our home for the night and a ride to town with us tomorrow." He glanced up at the darkening sky and racing thunderheads, "And this be a night for indoors, too."

Holding the protesting pig tightly Adam shifted from one foot to the other. He noted an amused smile on Kip's face. He was ambushed himself, for he could not escape these Quakers without being offensive. And a storm was gathering. In his irritation he squeezed the pig, which gave forth a loud squeal of anguish. Adam, looking rather sheepish, said, "Thankee, sir, I will stay the night."

Indoors, Tranquility was a sedate Quaker girl, demure, clean, and busy with supper. Yet, in spite of himself, Adam observed that her cheeks were still flushed and the long brown braid flopped angrily as she turned to the dutch oven, then back to the table. When they sat down to supper every head but Adam's was silently bowed in prayer. Kip's head was bent, too, but he glanced up at Adam's stiff neck.

"Eat hearty, lad," said Zack Willowby as he lifted his eyes. "My wife prepares vittles enough to feed Old Hickory's troops at New Orleans. Or all the uninvited borderers who swarm into the White House and muddy up the carpets for President Jackson."

Adam caught a fiery look from the brown eyes across from him. Was this girl angry at him because a stranger had seen her act with so little dignity? He scowled, then grasped his knife and began to shovel food into his mouth. Mouth full, he swallowed hastily as he looked around. The others were eating quietly, each using a fork, and the knife was employed only for cutting. Nobody seemed to take any notice of him. Nevertheless, beet red, he grasped his fork, speared a dumpling, and lifted it halfway to his mouth. Slowly he lowered it again and cut it into small pieces as he saw the others do. His rage rose into his throat, for he had not been taught manners in his apprenticeship.

"Now, let me tell you what happened to me in Burlington last summer," Kip was saying. "I had a promise for three portraits from Mr. Egerton, the rich importer of woolstuffs from England, and so I went there laden with paints and canvases. What did I find? You will scarcely believe this, Mr. Willowby. A lawyer from New York had been there, gotten friendly with Mr. Egerton's bookkeeper, and discovered some diddlings in the dealings — to cover up smuggling, you know. So he informed and brought government men down on Egerton. That respected merchant was taken to court for doing what many do in Jersey. It ruined him, lock, stock, and barrel. And so — poor Kip! No portraits were limned that trip to Burlington."

Adam asked slowly, his eyes alight, "Smuggling? You say many merchants — do they in Philadelphia, too?"

"Why, bless you, quite a mess of 'em do in the city, also. It's called 'trading' and nobody knows how many take it up. They do the states out of a pretty penny of revenue. It's a prime activity here in Jersey and has been since long before the wars. In those days it was patriotic to fox the British revenue officers. Now it's sharp business."

"Thee tells truth, Mr. Kip," said Zack Willowby. " 'Tis against the law, but some get off, even in court, for that law has more holes in it than did my old pantaloons when I arrived in these parts after fighting the king's troops."

"Then how did a soldier ever get to be a Quaker and a farmer? I've often wondered about that leather hat of yours."

"I wore it in the Battle of Bladensburg, known now jokingly as the 'Bladensburg Races' — but there was no joke about that engagement, not to one who fought there. I joined up to hold the British from burning the White House. That my joining did not prevent the disgraceful conflagration thee will not be astonished to learn."

Lightning flashed and thunder rumbled overhead, followed by a sudden downpour that drummed on the roof like musket shot. Farmer Willowby glanced upward, then continued, "I took that cap from a fleeing volunteer in the rout of our green militia, gathered to stop those solid regiments debarked from the British fleet. The volunteer flung his hat down on the road and ran away with the others like fleeing bucks. I picked it up, clapped it on my head, and went into battle with Captain Joshua Barney and his handful of brave sailors."

Willowby's voice was solemn and his eyes half-closed as he remembered the day. "There were a few of us left after the British marched on to Washington, and the Lord in his mercy spared me. Nearly all of those sailors died. I wear that hat to remind myself that I stood up to the redcoats."

"So, then how did you turn into a peace-loving Friend?"

"I wanted no more war — and Mercy here took me over."

"That was not so hard to do, Mr. Willowby," said his wife with a little smile. "Thee was already wanting to go back to farming as thee did in thy youth."

"Adam Quinn," said Zack Willowby, "is thee a Methodist shouter or one of them wet-headed Baptists?"

"No, sir — my mother was Quaker and my father Catholic. I am nothing at all."

In an uncomfortable silence his host said, "Well, then thee has quite a choice to make."

"Mr. Kip," said Tranquility, "thee is a smart man, clever enough to paint Friends here and there. Tell me, when thee stopped by last time, did not my father say he would let thee paint him?"

"Aye, Miss Tranquility, he did indicate so to me. I am right, am I not, Mr. Willowby?"

"Aye, so I did and so I will do, though my wife be contrary about paintings. She said she thought the Meeting would not like it, but I found that Hiram Joynas of Bogquake and his wife have been painted. My wife could say no more, not for me, although she calls out the troops, muskets at the ready, when it comes to allowing herself or Tranquility to be limned."

"Mother," said Tranquility with some heat, "thee need not be so firm about painting. Only the other day I saw a picture of Tabatha Hicks hanging in her parlor."

Mrs. Willowby, who looked so fragile that she seemed like a willow leaf trembling on a stem, drew her lips tight as she rose to clear the table. "Thee shall not have thy picture painted, daughter, not though every female in Friends Meeting does so. 'Tis vanity for a young girl."

"Ah," said Kip, "then why not you, Mistress Mercy?"

"No. Certainly not."

Kip glanced downward, and Adam's eyes followed his. Mercy Willowby, subdued in gray attire, wore shoes of the finest, softest leather. Adam thought she must have the smallest feet of any farm wife, or town lady, either, he had ever seen.

"Mistress Mercy," said Kip slyly, "just think how those dainty feet would look in a fine portrait hanging beside your husband's likeness upon the wall! In your Sunday velvet slippers with silver buckles, which I have admired."

She shook her head, and yet Adam thought he saw her glance down at her feet several times as she moved back and forth with her hands filled with dishes.

Chapter 4

A<small>DAM ROSE</small> from the featherbed as if he had slept on a cloud and found it hard to part with such rest. When he moved to the window and looked out upon a day fresh-washed by the storm, in spite of himself he began to whistle a lilting tune remembered these years from Patrick Quinn, the dashing Irishman. He was unaware that he was whistling until Kip's smiling face thrust around the door and he called out, "That tune sets me feet dancing, laddie."

Adam left off instantly and turned with a scowl. "I wish I were all Irish — and nothing Quaker in me, nothing at all."

Kip stepped inside and hastily closed the door. "Pull up there and down with that loud talk. You are not so rude as to want our good friends to hear you, are you?"

Adam clamped his jaws together and shoved back his hair with an angry hand. Kip hoisted himself to the side of the high bed and said soberly, but with a sharp glance, "It's good to be proud of your Irish blood, me laddie, and it's just as good to be proud of your Quaker heritage, too. Be fair and admit it's not right to blame all Quakers for the acts of one."

"Why not? They let my grandfather do what he likes and they but look the other way. They look on him with pride and say, 'That's Old Silver Cane himself! A great man.'"

"Adam Quinn, you listen to me. I'm a lot older than you are, me bucky laddie."

"Aye, but you aren't a hypocrite — doing one thing and saying another. Why do you take up for them?"

"There are all kinds, Adam," said Kip slowly, "all kinds of young as well as all kinds of old." He paused, then sent Adam a sideways glance, "Who is this grandfather of yours?"

"Who is he? Why, he's the most respected old man in all of Philadelphia. He owns shipyards and a fleet of ships that sail the seas of all the world. He pounds with his silver-topped cane and they all jump. Pious he is of a Sunday at Meeting — yet he bound out his grandson heartlessly to get rid of him. He gives to the charity hospital and to the orphans' home, but you cannot justify him to me."

"Don't shout so, or you will be heard below. So he is old Adam Jervis, but then I know him by that cane, as everybody does. It speaks louder than his squeaky voice. All Philadelphia knows it. My brother, Charles Lafitte the physician, knows him. There are dark stories afloat about Old Adam's past, stories of his slave ships 'black-birding' until stopped from bringing their human cargo into ports hereabouts. Once Quaker Meeting brought him up and near read him out of Meeting. But that was long ago, and forgotten by most. The old chap must be at least ninety by now."

Kip stood up, sniffing. "Come, I get wind of fresh bread and sausage. Forget your grandsire, Adam. You have a life of your own to look to."

Adam said nothing, but he still felt his anger surging up in him. He forced himself not to think of what he had done to his master, and he told himself that, since Old Adam had bound him out to Bolt Sherman, it was Old Adam's fault — not his own.

Breakfast over, Adam got silently into the spring wagon with the Willowby family and said farewell to Kip. It was hard enough to ride with Quakers, but to sit upon a plank laid across the back of the wagon sides beside a sturdy Quaker miss in Sunday dress was too much.

Tranquility, her braid pinned around her head under her bonnet, looked at golden bells blossoming along the roadside, and since her face was away from him, Adam allowed himself to send a sneaking glance her way. She turned quickly. He yanked on the lock of hair flopping over one eye and winced every time he thought her eyes were coming his way.

"Thee is thinking that in Philadelphia thee has not seen a Friend's bonnet pink-lined? We are not so staid as city girls."

Mercy Willowby looked over her shoulder reprovingly at her daughter, but held her tongue.

"What is that big hivelike thing?" asked Adam, getting up enough courage to ask a less personal question.

Mr. Willowby pulled in his horse to a slower pace as Tranquility replied, "That's a charcoal pit. Colliers who tend it must stay nearby all the time, night and day and even on the Sabbath, for the smoldering fire inside may burst out through those holes in wet clay covering. If so the charcoal is ruined. Bog raisers do not work on the Sabbath day, nor mill men, but coalers and furnace men must when the furnace is in blast."

Adam looked curiously at a man throwing a pail of water on one of the clay cones. They passed a second pit, now being torn down by a sooty man, while another loaded charcoal into a wagon box.

"See that coal box!" exclaimed Tranquility. "Smoke is coming from it. Those coalers are loading it before the charcoal is cooled. They will burn up the wagon box that way."

The worker turned with a surly look, shouting, "Never you mind, miss! This be our job, not yours."

Tranquility flushed, and her mother said sharply, "Daughter, I wish thee to remember thy name. And practice tranquility. Otherwise thee will go before Meeting for a public reprimand sometime."

"Remember my name? I wish I could forget it. It is a thorn in my flesh. Tranquility! I never liked it. Why could thee not have named me Mary Jane, or Elizabeth? I suppose I should be grateful that I am not called Tolerance or Suffrance."

"Daughter," her father's voice boomed out, "thee will not speak to thy mother in that angry way!"

"I beg thy pardon," she replied, but she did not sound as if she meant it. Then more quietly, "I did not realize that man could hear me."

She folded her mittened hands and bent her pink-lined bonnet over them. Her father swiveled about to look at her, frowned, then said softly to his wife, "Mercy — thee will do well to remember thy name, too, sometimes."

Adam stared curiously at the town as they came riding into it. A slow, brown river wound along one side of Bogquake, which was neither a bog nor yet was it quaking. He caught his breath with surprise at first sight of the principal street, for it was laid with crushed slag glistening blue, green, and silver in early sunlight. Houses were neat with flowers at the doorsteps and white-painted fences enclosing them.

Mr. Willowby turned around as they drew up before a small building. "Adam, if thee will go to Mr. Edwards, the ironmaster, and tell him I sent thee, he may likely give thee work."

"Meantime," said Mrs. Willowby, placing a velvet slipper with a silver buckle upon the wagon step, "for a place to live go to Mistress Anderson's boarding house. Yonder way it is at the far end of the street. She is a respectable woman who will put thee up."

"I thankee," said Adam, looking down, "for meat, and bed, and all."

The three turned away to greet their friends and go with them into the Meeting House. Adam moved slowly away, feeling more an outcast than he had felt before. Although Sunday in Bogquake was quiet with the furnace not yet in operation, there was a special noise of churchgoing made by arriving gigs, wagons, and carriages. There were also horses bearing Quakers from distant villages, some with feet and skirts splashed by streams they had forded to get there. The only other church in town stood near the

Quaker Meeting House. Adam guessed it to be Methodist, and he stopped to wonder at the bell installed in a belfry at the back of the roof instead of the front.

Among a throng of new arrivals Adam saw the finest carriage of them all, and in it the largest man he had ever seen. All turned to greet him,

"Good day, Ironmaster. How-do, Mr. Edwards, sir."

Adam backed off a little way to look as the ironmaster got down to help his wife and children from the carriage, and he thought that surely this man must weigh as much as a ton of bars turned out by his own works. Should he step up now, or should he try to see Mr. Edwards at his home after church? Sunday was not the time — and wasn't it likely that the man who owned the furnace would also be the magistrate of the town? Adam could not approach a magistrate. He did not dare.

As he walked along the street looking for the boarding house he saw a large house with a wing that had a sign saying, MATILDA FURNACE OFFICE. The mansion must belong to Mr. Edwards. It stood on a grassy slope where it could dominate the town. The walk leading to the door was bordered with hollies and laurels and was made of slabs of iron. The house itself was constructed of ironstone with reddish spots of metal dotting it like raisins in a pudding. Holding up the roof of thick cedar-shake shingles were posts that Tranquility had told him were iron pipes of the same kind made for the Philadelphia Waterworks System.

A huge buttonwood tree spread its branches over the house, which was surrounded by gardens, fields, and outbuildings. Behind it, in the distance, tall pines marked the edge of the forest. Servants moving about the place were both black and white, the whites he supposed to be indentured bondsmen and women brought from England to work out a term of service to pay for their passage. The sight of them reminded him of his own servitude, and he stepped back into the road suddenly, too miserable to watch what he was doing.

"Gorramighty! Git out of my way."

He leaped aside as a wagon driven by a rough-looking fellow nearly ran him down. Adam stood a moment after the wagon had gone, rubbing a finger over a callused palm, recalling that he had a trade and was good at it. He should be able to find a job somewhere in the ironworks, even without seeing Mr. Edwards. Now he must find a place to live.

At the end of the street the boarding house was set in a weed-grown field. Its windows stared at him above an open door as if daring him to enter. Adam approached slowly, knocked on the open door, and, seeing no one, he stepped into the hall.

"Who are you?"

A tall, raw-boned woman with a tucked-up apron over a purple dress glared at him. Her face could have been that of a man but for the cotton cap. She strode to the front door as if ready to toss the intruder out by the scruff of his neck.

"Well! Speak up. What you doing sneaking into my house?"

"Ma'am — I — I thought perhaps you could give me bed and —"

"I don't give anybody beds. I rent 'em. Who told you I would give you a bed?"

Adam glanced wildly at the open doorway but was

balked by the landlady who blocked it. He managed to pull his wits together.

"Mistress Willowby sent me."

The face softened slightly, "Zack Willowby's wife, the Quakers from out Long-a-Coming way? Well — they're decent folks. If they sent you, then come along, boy."

She turned like a drillmaster and marched up the stairs, her heavy shoes pounding bare boards. Adam followed, and then up another stairway to a big loft room, where wooden bunks filled with straw took up three sides of the walls.

"Take that one," she said, pointing at a bunk. "Bed fifty cents a week. Board one dollar. Both paid on Saturday night. If not paid out you go. Breakfast at four. Dinner at twelve. Supper at six. Take it or leave it, boy!"

"I'll take it, ma'am. I'm getting a job tomorrow."

"Wash down at the pump. Clean towel every Monday. Soft soap five cents extra."

She wheeled about, nodded her cap violently, and marched down the stairs. Adam went to his bunk and dropped down on the straw. Once he got up and then sat for a long time looking at a locket and thin gold chain, so fragile on the palm of his hand. He slowly stood, and carefully wrapped it again in his extra shirt, putting it back in his knapsack. As he stretched out on his bed he reflected that all he owned in the world was his extra shirt and hose and his father's battered British campaign knapsack containing the locket that dashing Patrick Quinn had given his bride.

In the distance the town bell on the Methodist Church rang, followed by the clanging of the supper bell below. Adam went down to the backyard to wash up. At first he stood back, nervous in this crowd of strangers. Would anybody suspect him? Had a notice been posted offering a reward for his return? These men paid him no attention at all as they shoved heads and hands under the pump.

"Get in line or you'll never have a wash."

The man behind him gave him a friendly shove and moved forward to pump a gush on Adam's hands.

"Name's Charley. Who be you?"

Adam rubbed his dripping hands over his face and then shook them, for he had forgotten to get his towel from the hook beside his bunk.

"Adam. I'm looking for a job."

"Well, shake a shin there, Adam, or you'll miss your vittles." So saying Charley made a dash for the dining room with Adam following. The long pine table was already half empty of food, and it did not take Adam long to understand that here he need not watch his manners. It was every man for himself, and the last one at the grab went hungry.

That night he dropped onto the straw in his bunk with eyes closing as he landed. It seemed only a few minutes later when, in thick darkness, a bell clanged loudly below. He sat up so suddenly that he banged his head on the bunk above. Feet hit the floor.

No time was wasted over breakfast, and Adam, stuffing bread into his mouth, joined the crowd hurrying to their jobs in the scattered buildings of the ironworks. He approached the smithy apprehensive over not having working papers and had no sooner asked for work than he found he need not have worried. There was no job open there. The head smith shook his head and said "Maybe later on?" As Adam turned away he called after him, "Try the forge."

The forge was quiet, waiting for the furnace to go in blast. Adam asked of a worker standing near and was told that there were no jobs open there either, but to "try the stamping mill." When he had made himself heard there above the noise of the great hammers he received the same reply. Everybody who could was moving toward Matilda Furnace on the bank of the river, and Adam slowly followed. He stood with some young boys watching.

"What's going on?"

The boy stared up at him as if he gazed at a simpleton. "She's going in blast. She'll not stop working till they put her out of blast for the winter, not unless she makes a puff and stops. Then they'll put her right back in again. You don't know nothing, do you? You must be green. Where you come from, anyhow?"

Adam turned abruptly and climbed the hill into which the furnace building was built. From the top he looked down on Sleeping River, where docks were lined with clam and fishings boats. Sloops from Philadelphia, by way of Delaware Bay, Adam supposed, swung lazily at anchor, alongside schooners waiting to take on cargoes of iron products to carry across the sea. He saw the huge water wheel turning a brown stream into a cascade of silver just below him, where it made power for Matilda Furnace. Adam thought that it must be when this wheel froze that the furnace went out of blast, to come in again with the first spring thaw.

He turned the other way to see box wagons filled with charcoal, and others with clam and oyster shells, moving forward in a long line, and he watched as they wound slowly up the hillside. He heard the shells called "flux" and saw them wheeled in barrows along with the same amounts of ore and charcoal to the gaping hole near the top of the stack.

"Out of the way!" shouted a foreman, giving Adam a shove. He moved back to watch the fillers rolling their barrows rapidly onto a wooden platform leading from the hilltop to the stack. Each time a filler dumped his charge into the hole of the pyramidal stack he ran back for more. Avoiding the sweating workmen, Adam threaded his way through the watchers down the hill and moved forward among wagons below to the casting house beneath the stack. He stood looking at the building, where already intense heat poured out and workmen were preparing for the first red-hot flow of molten iron, and decided that those two stoppered holes must be for the iron and slag to run out.

"Look alive there, Lem," shouted the red-faced furnacemaster to a man smoothing out trenches in the sand with a rake. "You get a-going. When we pull that plug them pigs and sow better be ready."

"What does he mean by pigs and sow?"

A man beside him said, "Them little sideways trenches head up to the big 'un like pigs feeding on a sow. You come back here tonight and you'll see pig iron molded." He squirted tobacco juice over Adam's boot and turned away. The furnacemaster was coming outside, so Adam went up to him.

"Can I get a job here, do you think, sir?"

"Go to the ironmaster's office if you want work."

Adam turned silently away and walked slowly along the street. As he passed Friends Meeting House he saw a young woman clad in gray step outside between two files of girls and boys. She was ringing a hand bell. The lines broke, the bell stopped ringing, and the children separated into laughing, shouting groups.

"Why, good morning, Adam Quinn. How does thee do?"

Adam said nothing.

"Why, does thee not know me?"

"I'm sorry, Miss Willowby. I — I was taken by surprise. I thought this was your church."

She came toward him. "So it is — both school and Meeting House. Friends believe in schooling, and we do not scorn lessons for girls, neither. We teach all the children of the town whose parents want them to learn, whether Friends or not."

Adam drew his upper lip betweeen his teeth.

"Did thee find a job?"

"No. There seems no place in this town where I am wanted."

"Has thee tried the forge and Matilda Furnace?"

"Aye, and the mills, too."

She frowned as she thought, hand to cheek. "Come in, Adam. We will talk about this."

He followed her into the school. Tranquility seated herself behind her teacher's desk opposite the door and Adam noticed that the pink-lined bonnet hung carelessly on a hook behind her. He edged past the stove and sat on a bench in front of her as if he were one of the pupils ready for the slate and the *Blue Back Speller*. He was so uncomfortable that he glared at her.

"Now, Adam," said Tranquility, "tell me why thee is so dreary. Did thee not see a sign in the store window asking for a clerk to keep accounts? Is thee above selling cornmeal and molasses?"

"No — no, I am not. I cannot be a clerk." His voice

was sullen, and this was spoken with head down.

She stared at him a puzzled moment, and then she said, "Ah, Adam, thee cannot do that work. Do not be shamed. Is it because thee cannot figure well enough? That's not so much. Thee will be taken on, anyway. Mr. Tower, the storekeeper, expects to train an account keeper."

"No. I can't." His throat was so tight that his voice came in a growl.

"Why not? Thee is a stubborn fellow. Why not try?"

Adam took a long breath and said in a desperate rush, "I work with my hands. I cannot —"

Tranquility frowned, perplexed enough to stare at him awhile. Suddenly she nodded, eyes on her own hands folded on her desk among books and papers, and said slowly, "Is it that thee has not yet learned to read?"

A glance at his face gave her the answer. "Why did thee not learn? Many apprentices have in the contract an agreement that the master must at least put them in school for reading and writing."

"No, not I." Adam cast aside all caution, wishing only to get talk over and go away from this prying girl, who made him feel like a stupid little boy. He stood up so abruptly that his bench fell over with a crash.

"I can't read. Do you want to know why? My grandfather bound me out to a blacksmith without that provision."

"Oh, is that so?"

"Aye. It's true."

"Didn't thee have a father and mother, Adam?"

"My mother died when I was seven. Her Quaker father disowned her because she married an Irish soldier." Adam's loud tone sank lower, although his anger was there. "My father went out into the West, saying he would send for me. He believed my grandfather would care for me in his home. Now my father is dead."

"That is hard on thee, hard indeed."

Adam glared at her. He wanted no sympathy, but only justice and a chance to work out his own life. She paid no attention to his anger. "Thee can learn to read." Suddenly Tranquility looked up at him and smiled. "I know what thee can do for a job for now. Mr. Hobson, the master ore raiser, will take thee on for a hand. He is always in want of men to dig bog ore and since it is hard, weary labor, not many stay on that job. If not scornful of hard work and wet feet all day thee can get work with him."

Adam drew in a long breath, let it out with a sigh, and said a short, "Thank you, ma'am," and started toward the outdoors and sound of children's voices in a game of crack-the-whip.

"Wait, Adam!" called Tranquility, rising hastily. "Tell Mr. Hobson I sent thee. Adam — hold a minute!"

He paused just inside the room, saying nothing.

"And Adam — if thee will come to the Hobson house where I live during the week, each evening, after supper, I will teach thee to read. If thee really wants to learn."

Chapter 5

THAT EVENING Adam presented himself to the master ore raiser, who was sitting on a bench outside his front door smoking his Dutch pipe.

"Can you use me for ore raising, Mr. Hobson, sir?"

A long silence in which the master ore raiser looked at Adam, who was shuffling one battered boot and then the other. Mr. Hobson slowly removed his pipe from his mouth as he said, "Ore raising be a man's work. Thee looks strong enough. Can thee stay with it? That's the question. How old is thee?"

"Fifteen, sir. I've done man's work these past four years and more. I'm a skilled ironworker and smith, but there seems to be no job open to me here."

"Ummm — well — we do not take boys on this job.

Tranquility has just now told me thee is capable, she believes, of doing good work." A twinkle appeared in his eye, or so Adam suspected, although he could not be sure of it. "How she could know I know not. Yet thee is a friend of Mr. Kip, too, she says, and that is a recommendation. So I will give thee a try. Come to the landing on the morrow."

Adam was the first worker down before dawn next day, and he went with Charley to the boat landing. Mr. Hobson was already there giving the day's instructions to his three work crews.

"So thee knows Charley Coons, Adam. Charley, thee will take on showing Adam Quinn how to go about the work and stay beside him for the day. Now, Ned, thee is to take thy crew up Bear Claw Creek to the place where it flows into West Bog, then move over to the right bank, there to work for this day. Adam, thee can take an oar."

Adam jumped into the long ore boat beside Charley and took hold of an oar. As they swung out into Sleeping River Adam pulled so heartily that the other oarsmen yelled at him and Charley shouted, "Ease up there! You'll send us up against that schooner. You got to pull in time with the others. Take it slow and easy, lad."

By the time they had reached the rusty brown earth of the bog Adam's arms ached from his first long stint of rowing. Yet that, he soon found, was a soft job compared to the work of digging heavy, wet, iron-encrusted earth and loading it into the boat. At noon as he dropped down beside Charley and opened his lunch pail, he wondered whether he could keep this up every day — and yet he knew that somehow he had to do it. Charley glanced at him and laughed.

43

"Ain't so easy, is it? You got a job, howsomever, so long as you can last it out. This is the lowdownest job in Bogquake. Looked down on by everybody, even colliers at the charcoal pits. Have you tried for a place in the smithy? Master Hobson said smithing be your trade. Well, that's a cut above coal burners, and nearabout on a level with top furnace and mill men."

"No job open for me in my trade. You been here long, Charley?"

"Aye, nearabout three years. I reckon I'm the onlyest bog raiser been here that long. Some leave after a day, some after a week, and the oremaster has to keep going to the city to bring out more. He's a patient man, Mr. Hobson is, and a good thing, too. And he's fair — that I'll say for him."

"Why do you stay? Why don't you get a job in the furnace or a mill?"

"Me? I never cared to. I got my reasons. Me and the oremaster are friendly, and he overlooks a few little lapses of mine, now and again. He don't fault me out loud for liking me bottle, anyways, not to the point of sending me packing, as some would do."

At the end of that first day on the job, Adam could scarcely stagger to the boarding house, boots dripping mud, body on fire with burning muscles. And yet, after a few days, he hardened up and was able to do almost as much work as Charley, who grinned at him and said he had given Mr. Hobson a good report of the new chap.

On the fourth evening, after supper, washed and in a clean shirt, and with mud scraped from his boots, Adam got up his courage to start for the Hobson home. On the way he passed men entering the taproom of the Bearshead

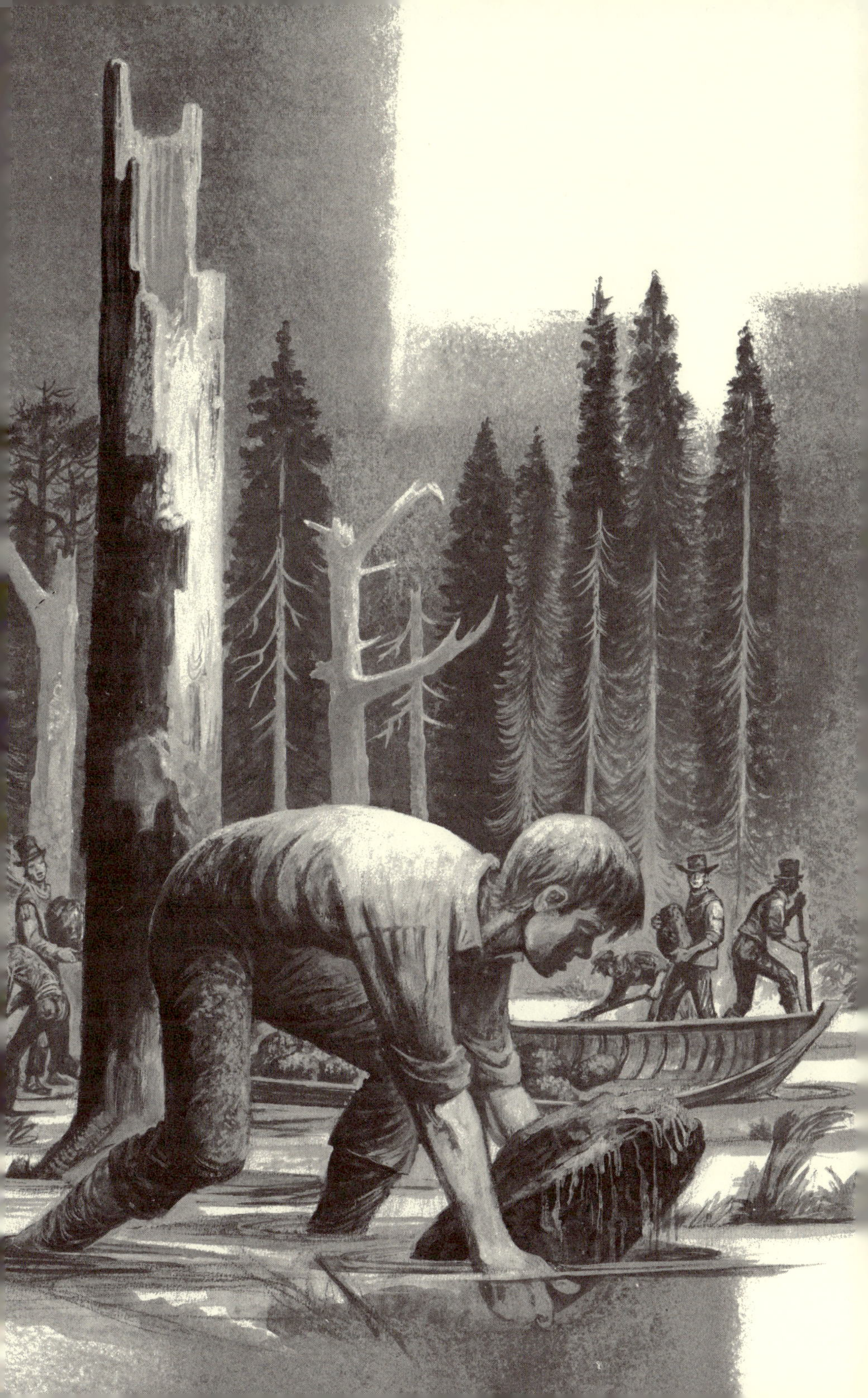

Tavern and saw others slumped on their front porches trying to catch a stray breeze from the river. Always, by day and by night, in this town there was the roar and blast of the furnace. These workmen were all pale and sweating at the day's end, and Adam had learned to raise his voice when he spoke to an older man, for he was sure to be stone deaf.

He came in sight of the Hobson house. It was larger than most of the others, and had a more plentiful plot of ground around it. Adam wondered at his own courage in coming at all. He had not thought he could take lessons from a girl. His success in digging bog ore must have stiffened his nerve as well as hardened his muscles, he decided, even as his steps slowed, and he debated whether he should turn around now and go back to the boarding house.

As he entered the open door, Tranquility called out from the scullery. "Adam Quinn! Is that thee?"

Her smiling face appeared in the other doorway, turning Adam red and embarrassed. "I'll be there in a moment for the lesson. Sit thee down."

The craggy face of the Quaker oremaster lifted from the ledger in which he wrote his log for the preceding week.

"Welcome, Adam. Charley tells me thee is doing well in the bogs. Is thee a drinker, Adam?"

"No, sir. A glass of ale now and then, but no more. I never took to it much."

"I am glad to know it. Drink is the curse of Bogquake and iron men." He sighed. "Listen to this." Slowly he read aloud, " 'Jos Williams drunk, fell in the mill pond and drowned himself. Charley Coons off with drovers to the shore on the Sabbath. Came back rum-soaked. No work out of him for the next day. Si Bates hanged himself, but not long enough. Back in the bog and not much good. All hands to Tavern for Militia Drill, which was more swilling than drilling. Ore boats idle this day.' Too often I must go and look for more men to dig bog ore."

"How did iron get into earth in bogs, Mr. Hobson?" Adam sat on a bench and stretched out his long legs. "Why do we go farther each few days to find it?"

"We're using it up fast all around here and must keep looking for more deeper in the barrens." He frowned. "On the morrow I will go out searching for a new untouched bog. I think soon I will have to get some ore wagons out, too. Some bogs cannot be reached by streams big enough to float our boats. As for how iron gets into bog earth — Mr. Edwards says rainwater soaking through pine needles and fallen trees leaches out iron from the sands below, and it washes into bogs in gravel and mud. It makes good iron, that it does, for bog iron never rusts."

Mrs. Hobson came from the kitchen and handed a wedge of apple pie to Adam, who said, "I thankee, Mistress Hobson, but I have had my supper."

"Food at Mistress Anderson's isn't fit for man or beast." As he ate the pie she beamed down on him. Tranquility laughed as she pulled down her sleeves and buttoned her cuffs after dish washing.

"Thee might as well learn at once that Mistress Hobson is not to be denied." When he had finished she took away the plate and on the table set before him a slate, a stick of chalk, an eraser, and an alphabet book.

"Now, Adam, when thee has learned letters and to write thy name, I will give thee foolscap and quill to use."

Adam gritted his teeth, grasped the piece of chalk in his big hand, and blushed to the roots of his hair when his teacher gently placed his fingers correctly around it. He hunched his shoulders over the table, lock of red hair in one eye, clutched the chalk tightly, and slowly copied a large *A* on the slate.

"Now, say the letter. *A* is for Adam."

On that he nearly choked and thought that he had rather work in wet bog forever than come to such as this. Yet he was more ashamed of giving up, with these three watching and listening to him. He had to remind himself that he had a plan for his life, unformed though it was as yet, and that plan required knowledge. When an hour had passed, and he had written his full name on the slate many times, he unloosed his stiff fingers from the chalk and sat back with a sigh.

Tranquility said, "Adam, thee is learning very quickly. Reading and writing will be most easy for thee." Eyes as well as lips were smiling.

He allowed a small grin to cross his face as he said, "Miss Willowby, you're a good teacher to bring such a lunkhead so far tonight as to write his name."

"Call me Tranquility, Adam, and no nonsense about it." She sounded annoyed. "And thee is not a lunkhead, neither."

With her rising irritation he felt more at ease. Even bold enough to say, "I'll try to call you that, but somehow it seems not to fit you too well. How about Quillie?"

Mr. Hobson laughed, and his wife said, "Calling her Quillie will get thee in badly with thy teacher. She dislikes that name above all things, you know."

"Nobody with your temper, Quillie, should be called

Tranquility, as you yourself said not long ago, and in my hearing. What other name is there to call you by? Quillie it is." His look was solemn. She frowned angrily, caught a hint of amusement in his tone, and said, "Very well then. But let that not make thee too confident, Adam Quinn, or thee will get a bad mark with me."

Surprised that he had so far unbent as to be able to joke with her, Adam found himself happier for the change. He had jumped the first hurdle to his plans, small though it was, and he would keep on going. Striding along the sparkling road in moonlight on his way back to the boarding house he softly whistled "The Irish Washerwoman" and forgot his still somewhat sore muscles and aching back. Under his arm he carried a battered, torn reader, one that his teacher had said was put aside to be discarded. As he left she had told him, "Thee may have this book to keep. I am sorry not to have a better one, but Bogquake Friends Meeting owns the school books, so I must account to the governors for each copy and each piece of chalk. Friends care greatly for education," she said with a laugh, "almost as much as they care for making money."

As Adam went out he heard Mr. Hobson's disapproving voice, "Tranquility, thee must not make jokes about Friends. Not in that way. Thee knows better."

Passing the lighted tavern, one of his fellow boarders came out and walked beside him.

"Mickey Flannery is me name, and you be Adam Quinn, I hear. Me father once had a kinsman named Quinn. Be ye from Cork, me boy?"

"No," said Adam, "I was born in America."

"Ah — and so was I, so was I — yet Irish is in me bones

and me blood. Didn't your mither and father keep you up with the Irish?"

"No," said Adam shortly.

"Judging by the sour look of ye, Adam Quinn, you be more English than Irish, and may the divil take a man denying his blood and his name!"

After that Adam was let alone by most of the men but Charley, who defended him in his easygoing way and was always friendly on the job and at the boarding house. Since Adam never joined in the amusements of the young men of the town, he was ignored by the workmen. They thought he considered himself above them. He felt sore at this but told himself he must not put himself in a position where he would be questioned. As soon as he had some money in his pockets, and knew how to read and write, he would head north to carry out his plans, which were still vague as to method, but hard and resolute in purpose.

So Adam went to bed on his pile of straw with the book beside him. The other workmen were snoring. He was not at all sleepy, and he clasped the little reader with eager hands; in the moonlight he studied the already familiar letters and slowly figured out "cat," "dog," "apple," "girl," "boy," until his head dropped on the page and he slept in spite of himself.

On Saturday Adam stood in line to receive his wages. He got a slip of paper with his name written on it, and the amount of his pay figured at seventy-five cents a day. He puzzled over it. That made how much for his six days of hard labor? He slowly ran his finger over the writing, and the sum, and finally decided that it was four dollars and five-ought — that made four and a half dollars. Seeing him in such confusion, the young fellow behind him said, "You take this paper to the store. They give you some of it in money. Some you have to spend in the store. Understand?"

Adam thought that he didn't understand too well, but he went with the others to the store. There he bought a blue osnaburg shirt, a pair of butternut brown pants, and new, heavy work boots. He felt more confident of escaping the notice of passing strangers when he had discarded his worn apprentice outfit. This left him just enough to pay his board and bunk rent. At the boarding house door he lined up to drop coins into the outstretched hands of Mistress Anderson. She stood in the doorway barring the entrance of those who did not pay, letting the others sidle around her. When she moved aside for him Adam could hear the money jingling as she dropped coins into her sagging apron pocket.

The month passed, the full moon diminished, and he could no longer make out the words in his book, which he pulled from beneath the straw each night as he went to bed. With his second week's wages he bought a tiny night light, one that was nothing more than a small iron saucer of tallow with a wick thrusting up, and a tinderbox to strike a light. These he hid with his book, ready for use when the exhausted men slept, with their bullfrog chorus of sound rivaling strange noises in cedar bogs on a windy day.

He lit the little wick and placed the saucer on his open book. Thus he read letters — then words, then numbers, then sentences and paragraphs — over and over until his eyes nearly closed and he had to blow out the flickering flame and hide the saucer.

Adam was not so tired from his work at day's end as he had been at first, and he joked and laughed with the Hobsons and Tranquility more often. Once he overheard Mrs. Hobson say to her husband that Adam Quinn's face had a sparkle to it, now that his eyes were happier, and his long upper lip no longer made him resemble a sad cow in a downpour of rain. This made him wince, but he could not be offended at Mrs. Hobson.

He listened when Tranquility put books aside to talk of her dream and her ambition to go as missionary to the Indians on the border. Since childhood she had wanted to do this, she said. There were other Quaker women who had done so, and she especially admired Ann Austin and Mary Fisher, both of whom had been persecuted in England for their faith and had come to wild America to convert and preach. She told him of the founders of her faith, of English George Fox and William Penn, and of John Woolman, of Mount Holly, who had been the leader of the Jersey Quakers.

But after a certain amount of this kind of talk, Adam grew restive in spite of his effort not to show his dislike for the Quaker faith, and at last he could not stop himself from interrupting her.

"I know something of another kind of Quaker. It was my pious grandfather, Adam Jervis, who bound me out and made no provision to allow me to be taught reading and writing."

She stared at him in surprise, "Is thy grandfather Adam Jervis of Friends Meeting in Philadelphia?"

"Yes — you have heard of him. I suppose everybody has. He's so well known for his gifts to charity." His voice was scornful.

She bit her lip thoughtfully, frowned and doubled up a fist, to put it down so firmly on the table that the chalk jostled to the floor. "Adam, I do not believe thee is fair to Friends. And, although I know some think too much of money and good living, I cannot believe a man high in Friends Meeting as Mr. Jervis is would be as bad as thee makes him out to be."

Adam got up suddenly, toppling his bench over. His face was white, eyes hot, lower lip thrust out.

"You know nothing about him!" he shouted. "Aye, he gives his ill-gotten gains to the hospital. And to the orphans' home. Yet his own grandson, also an orphan, he put out of his house."

Tranquility bent her head and picked up the chalk. She stood the bench upright. Then she smiled at Adam, saying gently, "Sit down again. I did not know what I said. And yet, though thy grandfather be the very old Beelzebub himself, thee should not be given to such rages. Thee will destroy thyself with rage if it burns so fiery inside."

After a while his face softened, and at last he said in his old teasing way, "Quillie, you are not the one to chide me, now are you? How about you? You have no temper at all, have you? You are as calm all the time as a clam in mud. When I misspell a word I have to jump for fear you will whack me over the fingers with a birch switch. Now you know why I spell so well. I'm scared to death of you, teacher."

Tranquility turned scarlet, and then took a deep breath. "If thee expects that, then thee will get that!"

She grabbed a birch twig broom from the hearth, and to the scandalized cries of Mrs. Hobson and a low chuckle from Mr. Hobson, Adam fled the house with his teacher laying the broom to his shoulders. As he made for the road he turned to see Tranquility standing at the gate laughing.

On the way to the boarding house he slowed to a walk, feeling the furnace heat, seeing the glow from the stack reflected on the shiny road. Mills were silent; there was no medley of sounds from smithy, street, and riverboats. Matilda Furnace had the town to itself, and all night long the place shook with the roar and blast.

Adam did not study that night, for he lay sleepless a long time on the straw. Talk of Old Adam had brought a terrible memory that he had to live through once more. That morning, on the day before he had fled the city, he had worked as always in Sherman's Forge and had been surprised when a messenger brought a letter. Mrs. Bolt Sherman had read it to him in her shrill voice, her only comment, "Nobody ever believed he would come back for you, anyway." Then she had thrust the paper at him and gone back into her house.

He knew every word of that letter by heart: "To Adam Quinn, This is to inform you that your father, Patrick Quinn, is dead. Respectfully yours, John Winston, Chief Clerk of the Jervis Shipping Co."

Adam had stared at it with unbelieving eyes for a long time and had then run through the streets to the counting house belonging to his grandfather. Behind his closed eyes he saw again the scared faces of clerks, with Old Adam pounding his cane as he ordered his grandson out of his sight. Spare and ancient, but strong and invincible as the devil himself he had seemed.

"Like father, like son!" he shouted, as he struck his cane on the scarred boards.

Too angry to be afraid, desperate enough for anything,

Adam had demanded to know how his father had died, and where. At last, without an answer, and the clerks all converging on him, he had flung out of the place and wandered the streets until very late at night, when, mind made up, he had returned to his master's house to get his father's knapsack and run away. Now a sickness settled into his stomach as he recalled what had happened then.

For as long as he lived and worked there he had expected his father to come for him. And when he had received no word from the western wilderness, Adam had determined to run away to find his father. He was only waiting until he knew his trade so well that he would not be a burden to Patrick Quinn.

Then the horrible thing had happened. He still did not know whether in his wild fury he had meant to do it. All he knew was that one moment he was trying to walk out of the house, and the next moment his master was barring his way with arms out at the top of the stairs. Adam had given a mighty push — and had watched as Bolt Sherman rolled down the stairs to the bottom, where he lay outstretched in a strange, contorted way, his long white shirt and cap looking like a funeral shroud.

Adam ran down and to the door, where he turned to see Mrs. Bolt Sherman leaning over her husband, screaming, "My God in heaven, he's dead — dead! You killed him. You killed him!"

At the top of the stairs the apprentices and the journeyman printer were staring down in horror. Adam ran. He ran in the streets until he couldn't breathe, and then he walked, gasping, until day came and he could get across the river. He realized they would look for him on the western road. So he would go over the river to Jersey —

where ironworks were — they wouldn't think of looking for him there — yet he must hurry — run again — even now they would be after him.

So here he was, safely in New Jersey, living and working in Bogquake. Now he must think of nothing but getting to New York City. And after that — somehow — some way — he would return to destroy Old Adam, and the whole Jervis family as well. He fell asleep desperately living his dream.

Chapter 6

ONE NIGHT Charley Coons, unexpectedly awake, growled, "You put out that light!"

Next day he spoke to Adam with some irritation as they jumped into the empty ore boat at the wharf, "Adam, don't you be putting light to that candle again. For a minute there I thought some thief was in the room. You wake those fellows and they'll beat you good."

Adam did not forget, but after a few nights he thought he could get away with it again, since Charley had not told on him, and wouldn't, he figured. So with great care he lit the tallow and got out his books. Tranquility, knowing nothing about Adam's late study, was astonished at the progress he was making in reading and writing. As for Adam, he was determined to study every night until, after three such nights, he nodded over his lessons and his teacher sent him home early to get some rest. She puzzled over his exhaustion but laid it to the hard work in the bogs that he did each day.

In his bunk that night he drew out book and candle and tried to learn, although his eyes kept closing until he jerked awake again.

"Fire! Fire!"

Adam was flung from his burning straw and dragged across the floor. Something fell beside him, and he grasped his boots. The whole garret rang with shouts as men beat at flames rising from the bunk. Adam got to his knees, groggy with inhaled smoke. Boarders from below tripped over him as they tossed pitchers of water on the fire. Flames hissed and died, and the fire was out in a smell of smoke, burned wood, and wet straw. The bare legged men in their blackened shirts shook their heads at the sight of scorched wall and ceiling.

"Who started this fire?" A great mountain of a lumberjack glared at Adam. "You, wasn't it?" He advanced, followed by several others, wiping their faces with sooty hands. Adam backed hastily toward the stairs, reaching blindly for the railing.

"You stop right there!"

He turned and found himself trapped between the angry men and Mistress Anderson.

"You — Adam Quinn, did you do this?"

Earlier he had seen the landlady rush to the burning bunk with a pail of water, but she had been too busy then to consider the cause of the fire. Coming up this time she was an advancing fury.

He stood dumbly on one foot and then the other as he

tried to pull his shirttails down around his legs. Suddenly Charley spoke. "Ma'am, it was an accident. No intention meant. He was reading by candlelight in the dark."

"Accident? Candle? You — you devil! You nearly burned my house to the ground. Get out! If I ever catch you around here again I'll have you run out of town."

The big man bellowed, "We'll do it for you, ma'am, tarred and feathered a-riding on a fence rail."

The landlady stepped past Adam into the room and marched over to see the amount of damage. Charley hastily shoved the knapsack and tinderbox at Adam, and said in a hoarse whisper, "Get going before they come at you again. Here — I pulled these out from under your bunk."

Adam took them thankfully.

"Wait!" screamed Mistress Anderson, beside herself with rage at sight of the charred bunk and wall. "You'll pay for this or I'll have the law on you."

With shaking hands he unloosened his knapsack from his arm, took out his savings, and handed them over. She counted the coins, grumbled at the small size of the pile, and pushed past him to march down the stairs. Adam ran from the house in his shirt, clutching his boots and knapsack. In the street he pulled out his old and ragged nankeen pants, now a tight fit and much too short, and put them on. With his knapsack on his shoulder he walked slowly along the street. The blast furnace roared, its light following his steps with a sullen, red glare. He came to Friends Meeting House.

There Tranquility found him in the morning, surrounded by wondering children. His head had dropped on his chest and he was sound asleep, one smoke-blackened hand on a battered leather sack.

"Adam! What in heaven's name has thee gotten into now?"

Adam shook himself awake, rubbed his numbed back with both hands, then got to his feet.

"I was studying in the night. So as not to awaken others I put my light on my straw bed, along with my book. I dozed off and first thing I knew Charley Coons was pulling me out of flames that shot to the rafters."

She laid a hand on his shoulder. "Glad I am that thee is alive."

"Nobody was hurt. The men put out the fire, but Mistress Anderson came and gave me a tongue-lashing. Then she took my money and threw me out."

"Adam, thee must go to the Hobsons' house. They like thee, and I will speak for thee. They will let thee have a home with them."

As he had walked the long street the night before Adam had thought he would have to leave Bogquake, and with as little money as he had brought with him. Now he began to feel that he had reached a turning point for the better. His life in the Hobson household, and with Tranquility Willowby there much of the time, was happier than he had ever known. He took to joking with them often and to teasing Quillie, who never again so far forgot her gentle raising as to chase him with the birch broom.

Instead she darted a sly taunt at him now and then, calling him a firebrand, asking how a city boy could ever have gotten used to hard work in the bogs. In return Adam made her flush by wondering aloud if she had caught a stray pig of late, and saying that in Philadelphia she would have been taught more deportment. At this Tranquility flared up, "Adam Quinn, do not think thee is the only one hereabouts who knows Philadelphia. I spent two years there in Mistress Fouler's School for Young Ladies, and 'twas a Friends School."

One evening Mr. Hobson came in, pipe in hand. He said to Adam, "I was over in Mr. Edwards' office today handing in my reports for the quarter. Jeff Turner, the master smith, was there along with some others. I heard him say one of his smiths has left. I told him thee could handle the work. How would thee like to shoe horses, Adam?"

"I would like it right well, sir. And yet — you are short-handed —"

"I'm always short-handed, and I could use thee."

The oremaster sat down at his desk and began to write in his log book. Adam's hopes died. He said nothing more. When the oremaster finished his writing he turned around, "Take a look at this notation for today."

Adam got up and went to look at the log, eyes slowly following the entries, thinking Mr. Hobson to be testing his reading skill.

"Furnace made a heavy puff on Wednesday last. Slowed up ore boats and wagons until fires were started and furnace was put in blast. Good supply of ore then brought in from Pennypot River. Mr. Edwards visited the wagon box crew working near Ong's Hat Settlement. Saul Timmens back from jail. Mistress Timmins made a muster and brought forth a fine boy of 8 lbs. and 2 oz. Saw and greeted the herb doctor, in town from the pine barrens, on his way to the city to sell his potions. Charley Coons drunk again. Missed ore boat today. Released Adam Quinn this night to start Monday next at the smithy, as that be his true trade. Plan a trip to the city Wednesday next to sign up four new raisers."

Mr. Hobson's craggy face had a trace of a smile.

"I told Jeff Turner he could have thee for the job at the smithy."

And so again Adam's hands clasped a hammer and his ears rang with clang of metal. His nose grew familiar with the odor of burning charcoal, hot iron, and sizzling horny hoof as he held shoe against hoof to test for size and curve. He could talk with more ease to the smiths than to ore raisers, and here he made a friend or two. Shoeing horses was not the job he meant to do all of his life, but it was easier than digging bog ore and he was a little proud of his skill in the smithy. And yet Adam's eyes still sought and searched out every stranger who appeared, and he let out a breath of relief each time he found the man to be unaware of him. He could not forget that seaman, and the way he had stared at him, and a shiver took him when he thought of him.

One night in September Adam was struggling with a school reader meant for older children, trying too hard, getting too anxious about it, feeling that he would never learn to read well. The next evening, while not really trying, Adam let his eyes follow the text of William Penn's *Account of the Rise and Progress of the People Called Quakers*, and suddenly, like a flash of lightning, he knew that reading was easy.

"Adam, thee is really reading!"

He put down the book and stared up at Tranquility beside him. Mr. Hobson congratulated him. Adam held the volume as if in a daze, face remote with his own thoughts.

"Could thee read so well and not tell us?"

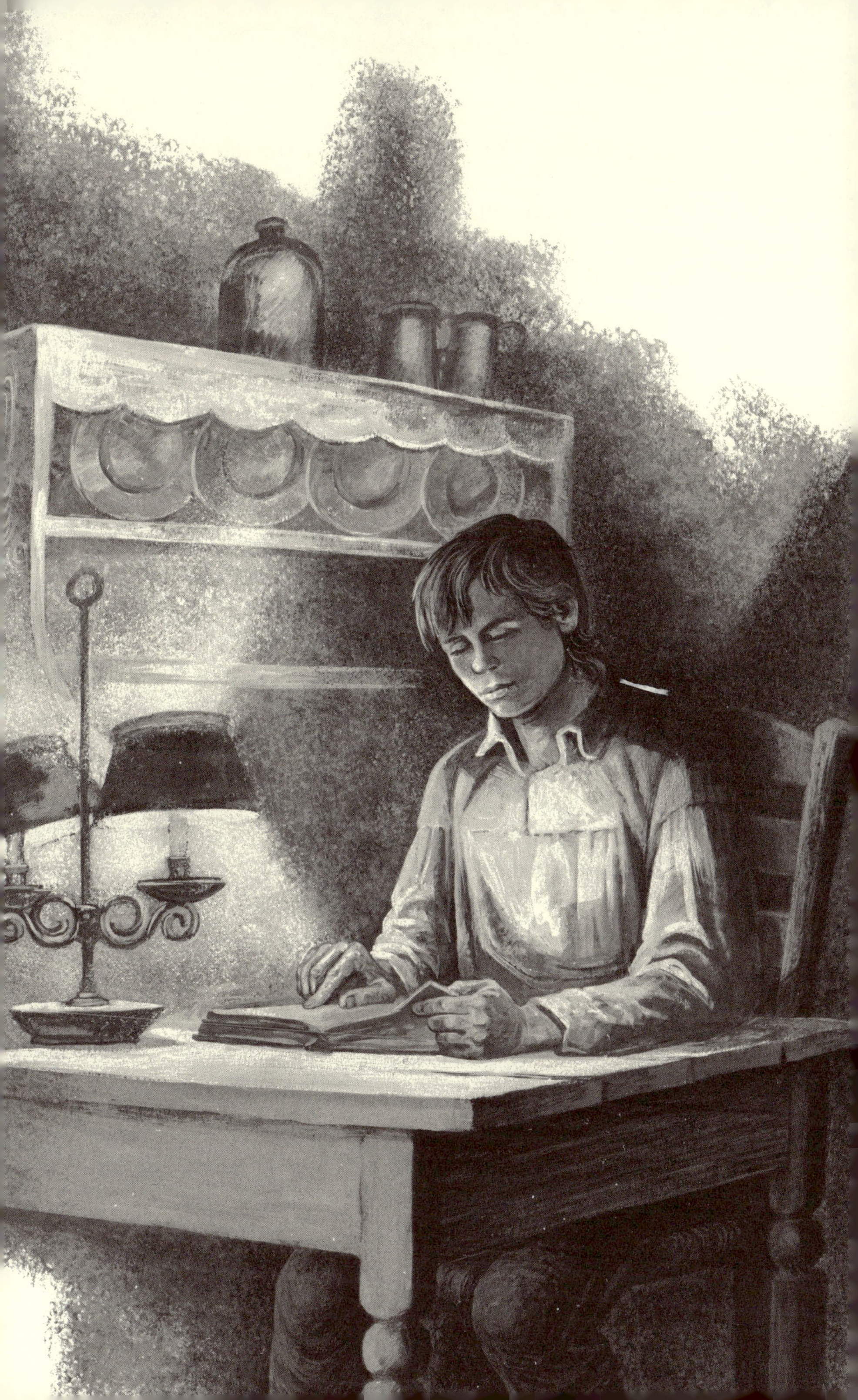

"No, Quillie, I knew no more than you did that I could do this."

She answered with a serious face, "Thee no longer needs a teacher, Adam. I want no more evening pupils, however, for indeed thee was a difficult student and I am wore out with the effort."

"Thee looks exceptionally wore out, Tranquility, just worn to a nub," said Mr. Hobson. "I think thy mother must be told to fill thee to the brim with sulphur and molasses on this Sabbath when thee goes home."

"Don't dare tell her that! Please do not, for even though sulphur and molasses is a spring tonic she would dose me till I could not bear it."

"Adam, why not go to the farm with me when I go on Sunday? Mr. Kip said he might stop by this week to see how the portraits of my father and mother look set in their frames upon the wall."

"Why not? I would like right well to see Kip again."

Then at Sunday breakfast Mrs. Hobson said with a look that was a little too indifferent, "Thee might go to Meeting with us, Adam, and leave with the Willowbys from there."

Adam dropped his fork. "I said I would go to the farm to see Mr. Kip. I didn't say I would go to Friends Meeting."

"Ah, lad, thee ought to do both," rumbled Mr. Hobson around a mouthful of corn cakes and honey. "Thee is expected to go with the Willowbys, so why not to Meeting?"

"No. I can't do that. I'll not go."

Three pairs of eyes studied him solemnly, then Tranquility said, "Very well, as thee wishes. If thee changes thy mind come to Meeting on foot. We know thee dislikes

Friends. We know thee is prejudiced against them and unreasonable about it. We don't expect thee."

"No — I am not unreasonable, not about all Quakers."

"Then thee is prejudiced only against our faith, and thee is burning up with rage at it."

"No!" Adam got to his feet, leaving his breakfast unfinished. "You are the one who is unfair. I am not that stupid. Yet, so long as Quakers admire and honor Old Adam Jervis I cannot have respect for Friends Meeting."

He swung around to the door and outside. Dressed as he was in his new black suit, muddying his newly bought boots that he had been so proud of only this morning, he strode across the garden and into one of the ironmaster's fields. He was scarcely aware of what he was doing. He forgot this was the first Sunday suit he had ever owned and that he had thought when he bought it that now he was a citizen of Bogquake and no longer would ever be recognized as a runaway apprentice. He had even been able to push his guilt back out of mind.

He walked through the cornfield, between rows of cut brown stalks, kicking a stone before him. Beyond the field golden birch and flaming maple quivered in autumn haze. For a long moment he stood still to watch Mr. Hobson bringing the carriage around from the stable, and the two ladies getting in with their gray silks and sober bonnets, and with fine dove-colored wool cloaks about their shoulders. They rode briskly away. Adam heard the Methodist church bell ringing with long, solemn tones, quite unlike its loud clang each morning and evening to call the furnace workers to day and night shifts.

He was his own man. He had nobody. That Adam told himself over and over. He didn't need anyone. These people were good friends but they had no right to rule him. And yet he owed them something. He would not set foot in Quaker Meeting, but he could join them and go to the Willowby farm to see Kip. He walked quickly and arrived just as the doors opened and sober folk emerged, to gather in small groups for a little talk and laughter. Adam waited uncomfortably, not quite sure that they would be pleased to see him.

Mr. and Mrs. Hobson greeted him with smiles, and Tranquility, following with her parents, had a triumphant look that irritated him unbearably. Behind her, through the open doors, Adam could see a little group of Negroes rising to leave the corner in which they had sat away from the white congregation.

"Adam, is thee going home with us for the day, after all?"

"Aye, if that be right with Mr. and Mrs. Willowby?"

"Glad to have thee, Adam, and so will Mr. Kip be, too." Zack was hearty and unconcerned, and Adam even received a gracious nod from Tranquility's mother. He climbed to the plank across the wagon and looked sulky, still annoyed at that triumphant look.

"Adam, thee missed a good service today."

"Did those black slaves sitting in the corner think it a good service?"

"Slaves? Of course they are not slaves," said Mercy Willowby from the front. "No member of Friends Meeting keeps slaves."

"Well, ma'am, that is what I thought. But those — they looked like slaves sitting off away from the others."

Before her mother could reply Tranquility broke in, "They are servants. They are paid for work by Friends.

Thee sounds as if thee thinks we are slave drivers and hypocrites. Shame on thee, Adam Quinn!"

Adam wished he had not opened his mouth to stir up such a storm. He could not imagine why he had done so anyway, unless it was because he had harbored a mean wish to get it back at Tranquility for that smile.

"Well, Quillie," he said, hoping to ease this into a teasing exchange, "I meant no harm. Don't be so easily offended. I just wondered — thought I would ask. You wish your old pupil to keep on learning, don't you?"

"Thee need not be insulting. I am not easily offended. Indeed, if I had been I would never have continued to associate with thee."

"That's enough, daughter," said her mother in a troubled tone. "Adam, we do not like the 'black corner' as it is called. I am trying to bring our people, at least some of them, to a better way of thinking, as the Grimké sisters are doing in Philadelphia. So far I have not succeeded. The vote is still for that segregation corner. I will do it in time."

Adam was embarrassed and could have kicked himself for making things so uncomfortable. They were all silent the rest of the way. At the farm he got out of the wagon still annoyed at himself. When he tried to hand Tranquility down she jerked away and jumped lightly to the ground unaided.

At that moment, while Adam was wondering whether he should leave right then and walk back to Bogquake in his stiff new boots, he heard a rattling and a jolting on the road. Around the turn, with a loud whinny, came an old mare at an unaccustomed speed. Rembrandt Kip was urging her on and shouting greetings as he drew up beside the wagon.

"As I live and breathe if it ain't Adam Quinn all gussied up for Sunday! Ladies, beautiful as always, how-de-do. Zack, you are well and prospering, to that I will swear, for you look like a farmer with hay in the barn and a good harvest ahead. Well! Goot, this is."

That cleared the air as if a thunderstorm had swept over and gone. They sat at table with platters of chicken dumplings and gravy before them, kept warm all morning in the dutch oven, and with fresh bread, apple butter, and all of the pickles and jams in jar or crock that the women could bring out.

"Vore o'clock, all's vell!" sang out Kip, sitting back replete with food.

"I'm surprised that homely old horse of yours can still pull the sheet wagon," said Adam with a grin.

"Hendrickje? She is in her prime, me lad — her prime of life. She may be ugly in the phiz and not so handsome in the withers, but she takes me and my sheet top right smartly along."

Kip sat and talked of his recent travels. He had gone up the main road through the barrens and turned to the shore, a somewhat different route than usual for him, he said, and then along the coast to Fork-ed River and Tom's River and across the pines country again to Mount Misery. Hoping to find new and untapped places for his portraits he had braved the dangerous barrens where pines robbers lurked.

"I will not go that way again, though," he said ruefully, "not because of attacks on my person or wagon, but for a better reason. I did not find many who wanted pictures. I met some strange folks on my way, and the strangest was a fellow named Garf. Seemed to me I had glimpsed him before, too, although it kreisseled me not to remember where. No matter. He had a fierce look, with a lid that drooped over a brown eye, and a wide open blue one. And when the lid popped up now and then, like a window shutter opening, it took getting used to, I'll tell you. All he said was that he was searching for somebody. Wouldn't say who or why. He was on his way to Martha's Furnace."

Adam felt his face tighten. "Is he looking for —"

"A cutthroat maybe?" said Zack.

Kip glanced at Adam curiously. "Seemed like it. Must be one of those bounty-hunting constables from the city. I was glad enough when I pulled into town and saw the last of him."

The remainder of his visit was a nightmare to Adam. When Zack showed them the two portraits on the parlor wall Adam was unable to say anything. He hardly glanced at the lady in gray with her elegant little feet.

At last, when Kip had said farewell for now, promising to return in the spring, Adam found a few moments alone with him as he was leaving. He stood beside the wagon, and Kip said, "Good luck to you, laddie."

Adam burst out, "Did that constable say where he was going after Martha's Furnace?"

"The man with the mismatched eyes? Aye — he spoke of heading from there to Allaire on the rim of the bog-iron country. Said he was trying all iron towns. Thought his quarry would seek out iron work — or blacksmithing.

"Said he's been this way already and is going on in other directions."

Adam sighed, and Kip added quickly, "Adam, Tranquility tells me you can read and write and figure some, too. 'That's a lad will make his way in the world,' I said to her. So goodbye, now."

Adam watched the dusty canvas top of the wagon move slowly toward Long-a-Coming and Camden. Then he gathered his thoughts and found little relief in them. In the farmhouse that night he slept fitfully and opened his eyes more than once in a cold sweat. At dawn he decided that he would probably be safer in Bogquake than elsewhere just now. He was not ready to carry out his own secret plans, and he must save some money for coach fare. And that man — he could be chasing another quarry, although Adam could no longer convince himself of that.

Chapter 7

"You are skilled. Where did you learn your trade?" asked Jeff Turner.

Adam struck the horseshoe a hard blow, then another before he said, "Philadelphia."

He wouldn't lie about it. He would keep his secret to himself, but he wouldn't lie about where he came from. Probably anyone could have known that anyway, from the way he spoke and looked. Jeff gave him a glance, nodded, and said, "You took good advantage of your training."

Several weeks passed and there was no sign of Garf. Adam's fear eased until once more he enjoyed his talks with the people he knew in the town. With another young blacksmith he went now and then for a mug of ale of an evening, or to a wedding party, and sometimes to a game in a field on a holiday.

Tranquility did not invite him to the farm again, but his evenings in the Hobson home were happy. Mrs. Hobson sat by the late autumn fire making patches for winter quilting bees. Mr. Hobson read, or wrote, as he liked so well to do, in his weekly log. With his small, precise handwriting, and in few words, he put down the joys and sorrows, births and deaths, workaday happenings, delinquencies, and the comings and goings not only of his own work crews but also of the townsmen and their wives. This he was not required to do, for Mr. Joynas, the ironmaster's manager and chief clerk, kept such a complete account of the Bogquake workers.

Tranquility sometimes corrected school papers, or sat and sewed or read. Adam always read, although now he had to reread the same books over, for he had exhausted the small supply.

"Adam," asked Tranquility one evening when they listened to wet leaves slapped on the windowpanes by the wind. "What does thee intend to do with thy life? Thee knows what I mean to do. I have told of it often enough. Thee has never said."

His eyes came up from Fox's *Journal* to fix themselves on her. He gave no answer. His face was tightly closed in against her.

"Well," she said, "thee need not say if thee does not wish to. 'Tis none of my business, heaven knows. I did think thee a friend who would talk to me. But maybe thee has no plan."

"I have my plans. I know what I mean to do. I will not talk of it, except to say that as soon as I have the money saved I mean to leave Bogquake for New York City. It is hard enough to get money put by here where pay comes in scrip."

He pulled a printed paper from his pocket. It had his name written on it in Jeff Turner's large handwriting, with the amount due him. "Here it says, 'The Matilda Ironworks will pay bearer on presentation the amount of Five Dollars in Goods at the Bogquake Store.' This isn't money!"

"Thee can take some of it in silver," said Mr. Hobson, "when presented at the store."

"Aye, that I do." Adam angrily crushed the paper in his hand, then smoothed it out again. "I do pay my board with silver, as you know. How much is then left? Twenty-five cents each week, and the right to buy goods with the remainder."

"Thee has a fine Sabbath suit, Adam, and warm clothing for working in the cold," said Mrs. Hobson.

Adam scowled. "I mean to save every coin I can earn."

"And after that?" asked Tranquility.

"After that I shall leave Bogquake."

"And after that?"

"Go by stage to New York."

"Why not to Philadelphia?"

"I have a right to keep my own counsel. I make my own decisions. Nobody can tell me what to do. And nobody can force me to tell more than I've told already!"

A heavy silence fell on them all. At last Tranquility said in a low, hurt tone, "We do not want to force thy confidence, Adam, if thee does not wish to tell us. This I do know — anything born of rage and hate burns the bearer up."

Adam got to his feet, thrust the book under his arm, and said a short "Good night." He lit a beeswax candle and stood for a moment with the small flame below his face. His eyes burned. He saw his friends staring at him sadly. In the upper hallway, hand on bedroom latch, he heard Mr. Hobson say, " 'Tis a good thing the chap took George Fox's *Journal* with him. It will give him peace."

"I misdoubt that," said Tranquility. "I do not think anything will. I know not at all what will become of him."

Adam did not want to overhear talk about himself, yet he was rooted to the spot. Mrs. Hobson sighed, "Tomorrow I must make a green tomato pie for Adam. It is his favorite. The lad needs to eat more."

"Why does he hate us, and all Friends?" exclaimed Tranquility, "when his own mother was of our faith?"

"He doesn't hate us. Leave him to God."

Adam opened his door, walked through with heavy tread, and slammed it behind him with a bang that shook the rafters. He wanted them to know he had heard them talking about him.

Leave him to himself. That was all he wanted. He could take care of himself. Nobody could tell him what to do with his life.

Holding out his hands he saw that they were shaking, and he put the candle holder carefully on the chest. Ashamed, hating himself but hating others more, friend and foe alike, he went to bed. And still that night Adam got little rest, for at intervals he jerked awake to see Old Adam's hawklike face, and every time sleep came he was jolted up again by the pounding of a silver-topped cane.

Following that night an uncomfortable silence fell between Adam and Tranquility, and then it eased off gradually, although they did not joke together so lightly as they had done before. One day she returned from the farm with several books in tattered leather bindings and handed them to Adam with a little smile.

"I brought thee these to read. My father sent them, thinking thee would like a change from Quaker pious works, or so he said."

Adam fingered them joyfully. His eyes devoured the titles — here was a collection of pamphlets by Tom Paine, written during the Revolutionary War — also a history of the French Revolution — and Ben Franklin's *Poor Richard's Almanack*, a book of poems, a sea captain's voyages to the Sandwich Islands, and Parson Weems's *Life of George Washington*.

As he read them friendship gradually returned between Adam and Tranquility. Autumn leaves came swirling into the dark waters of bog and stream. Icy winds of a nor'easter raged in from the distant Atlantic Ocean, sending cedars into wild lament, churning Sleeping River wide awake to overflow its banks. Overnight, winter struck on the heels of the big blow. Everybody huddled in wraps and spoke of how exceptionally cold it was for December, but said it wouldn't last. Nevertheless boots slipped and slid on icy patches and snow lay in thin streaks alongside buildings. The forge closed with a freezing creek and bog raisers found digging hard. When the furnace wheel could no longer provide power for bellows to pump air the furnace went out of blast. Adam's ears missed the roar and shaking, and the pounding of hammers in the stamping and slitting mills. Mr. Hobson's crews ceased to work and began to drift away from the town.

Adam worked as usual, for the smithy was still needed, although not at full strength, and two of the smiths had left with Charley Coons to find work for the winter months in Trenton. As his boot soles cracked on the slag road Adam reflected that he was lucky to be here with a job to do.

On the day Matilda Furnace died the whole town of Bogquake changed. Furnace slag cooled into a lump called a salamander, which would remain in the hearth until spring when it would be hauled out to join a pile of fellow salamanders near the creek. Workmen who stayed took on jobs readying the furnace and mill machinery for spring blast, repairing metal parts, and doing odd jobs of carpentry. Ice-cutting crews sawed and hauled frozen blocks from river to sawdust-filled icehouses, and men went into the woods to make new charcoal pits or cut timber. Yet the town was different with more than half of the men gone. Now days were counted until the frolic, always an event when Matilda went out of blast, and this year a double frolic with Christmas near.

Adam had not thought of going, although one of his friends teased him with, "Anybody would think you a sober-sided Quaker, though you say you are not."

"I am not." Not wishing to sound surly he followed this with a smile. "And I can't dance, John."

"Never you mind that. You can watch me do a buck and wing. I'm going to fling high, wide, and handsome."

"No, thankee. I don't think so."

He went slowly back to the Hobsons', which was dull this night without Tranquility, who had gone home to the farm. The bell was ringing joyously to call merrymakers to the Edwardses' big barn, and Adam thought he could hear fiddle music faintly. He could not keep his mind on his book. Suddenly he went upstairs, got into his new Sunday suit, and came down quickly. Why shouldn't he?

He found his coat and shrugged into it, saying, "I'm off to the frolic. Good night to you both."

The Hobsons looked up, startled, and nodded.

As he approached the barn Adam's spirits rose. The stone building was built into a hillside, with a lower level where cows were stalled and where horses moved restlessly with the noise overhead. He joined a pushing, joking crowd going inside and felt a wave of steamy heat envelop him. Dust rose around the boots of jigging men, who jumped into the air and landed with feet pounding. Some couples danced a merry reel at the far end of the room, and the air was heavy with applejack fumes.

The ironmaster and his wife never came to a frolic but had the big barn cleared for the blast-out event. They celebrated Christmas with a party in the mansion, enjoyed by the local physician, his wife, and visiting gentry. Adam sidled around the wall until he was near the fiddler, who was sawing away on a tune called "The Bailiff's Daughter of Islington."

"Yoweee!" shouted John, catching sight of Adam, who grinned and felt a tingle in his feet as he wished that he could dance. Glancing at the door Adam saw another crowd of men pushing inside. With a shock his eyes fixed on one. It was that burly fellow in seaman's clothing. Garf! Hastily Adam slid behind a tall lumberjack and peered around him. The stranger was slowly making his way into the barn. Panic seized Adam.

He gazed wildly around and saw the loft ladder nearby. He sprang up the ladder, oblivious to the fact that Garf might have noticed. Lanterns swinging on the rafters cast strange shadows back and forth on the rungs. At the top he crawled behind a pile of hay. A faint light came in through the open hayloft door along with the bitter wind. Adam buttoned his coat to the chin and pulled on his cap. There in the hay, in spite of the cold, he grew a bit drowsy. What was that? Every nerve in his body tingled. He could hear a slow scraping on the ladder. Somebody was coming up. He grasped at the thought that it might be a couple meaning to spark in the loft. Yet it didn't sound like two, and it was so stealthy. The noise ceased. Adam's breath left him in a hiss. There it was again! Sound of boot on rung. Then silence. The man had reached the loft.

Adam crawled rapidly to the hayloft door and thrust his head out. There was no moon and he looked a long way down into darkness. He could not judge how far the drop was, or what kind of ground lay below. The sky was a slightly paler background for a row of trees in the distance. His ears caught a shuffling behind him. He jumped — and went down into a black hole in the night.

He heard his left knee crack and felt it twist on hard earth. He picked himself up and in one motion, pain ignored, he was off into a clump of trees. Like a fox running from baying hounds he zigzagged into a patch of darkness that was deeper than the way ahead. He ran alongside a hen house, and then through yards and vegetable gardens, by sheer luck avoiding a fall. When he gasped for breath and had to stop because of the pain in his knee, he knew where he was. The night world was lighter to him and objects visible. It was not so far to the Hobson house. He listened, and heard nothing behind him.

As Adam limped into the dim house he told himself that he could escape — he was not trapped. There was no light but a dying glow from the hearth. He shivered uncontrollably and moved close to it and held out his hands to the dull red coals as he rested his weight on the good leg. He must hurry. Garf might know where he lived and how to find the house. Yet Adam paused a moment to look at firelight lying on the worn rug and caught in a pair of steel-rimmed spectacles beside a Dutch pipe on the table. Sewing was neatly folded on a low chair. His book still lay on the bench, opened as he had left it.

Pain shot through his knee and down to his foot. He hobbled up the stairs to his room and packed as many of his clothes as he could press into his knapsack. He removed his Sunday suit. It must remain here until he came for it, or until Mrs. Hobson gave it away, if he never returned, then drew on the old leather jerkin over his work clothing. It was the only garment from his apprentice days that he could still wear. After a little hesitation, he placed one of the books in his knapsack. He was troubled about taking Zack's book, but he chose the smallest, *Poor Richard's Almanack*, for he felt he needed a book of some kind for companion.

Then he reached into his knapsack and drew out the locket and his savings. He found a scrap of foolscap that was a lesson sheet he had kept because it was the first perfect writing that he had done. Three of the five coins he placed upon the table in candlelight. The thin golden chain he let run through his fingers as he looked down at the cameo. Since he could remember he had believed that the white face of the lady on the locket was his mother's portrait, but he did not know that it was. Adam turned it over to look again at the engraving on the back, running his calloused finger over the name — ABIGAIL JERVIS QUINN.

He went to his desk where he dipped quill in inkpot and wrote: "To Mr. and Mrs. Hobson. Thank you for all you have done for me. I am sorry to leave like this. I cannot return. Here is my week's board and rent. Your friend, Adam Quinn."

Hurriedly he dusted sand over ink and tore the note from the sheet, wrapping it around the coins, placing the package on the desk. Then he wrote again: "Dear Tranquility, Thank you for teaching me and for friendship. I am taking a book. I will return it someday, tell your father. This is for you. Adam." Wrapping the necklace tightly in the note he placed it beside the other.

Knapsack on his shoulder, Adam limped as fast as he could up the road. Drawing the collar of his coat about his ears, he pulled his cap down against the wind. Once he gave a glance at the teakwood dam, made from a foundered ship's hull, now encrusted with early icicles, and at the gristmill white with flour and frost beside Sleeping River.

Could he find a ship to take him on as a cabinboy and carry him to the far end of the world? Better to go on as he planned and try to reach the city called New York someday. Bitter rage rose in his mouth as pain swept down from his knee. He hobbled from Bogquake to the fork in the road and turned into a narrow strip of sand, creased by wagon tracks, leading deep into the mysterious pine barrens. The dark line of trees closed around him.

Chapter 8

AT FIRST Adam wanted the darkness to swallow him as he hurried into it. And yet, with steps growing more painful, time and again he had to sit down on fallen logs beside the road, glimpsed in light between black walls of trees. Pines sighed in a rising wind. Cold struck deep and a few snowflakes drifted into his face. Shivering, he got to his feet and limped on. He felt rather than saw a bog on his left and heard cedar boughs crying and moaning. Some said the devil kept his lost souls in cedar bogs.

Catching a whiff of pine beyond a bog just passed, he left the road and stumbled a little way into the forest. Dropping down on soft pine needles, with both hands he moved his left leg back and forth. Agonizing though it was, and already much swollen, he decided that the joint was not broken. He would gather sticks and make a fire. Why hadn't he thought to take food from the kitchen? They would not begrudge it to him. He felt around in his pocket once, twice, and then holding his breath he searched his knapsack. He had forgotten his tinderbox. In despair he drew himself into as much of a ball as possible, pulled his jacket tightly around him, and slept from exhaustion.

He awoke in terror. Jerking to his feet he heard a screeching, sobbing cry just above his head. A panther ready to spring? Adam had heard awful tales of panthers in the pines. In cold moonlight he saw two yellow eyes in the tree above his head. With a limping run he made off through the forest — dodging between tree trunks — stopping — running, his breath caught, then gasping out. He struggled on until he dropped and could run no more. When he breathed easier he realized, city boy that he was, that he had given way to sheer panic. Recalling all that he had heard from pineys who had come out of the barrens to work in the furnace town, Adam told himself, "That wasn't a panther. They scream, but not when getting ready to spring. It must have been an owl."

He forced himself to limp slowly on because, owl or not, he knew that bears and fierce wild pigs as well as panthers lived in this wilderness, and he could not even try to sleep again. Trees were thick overhead, yet shafts of moonlight struck through them now and then. He looked for the road and did not find it. At last he saw a faintly gray sky through sparse trees and sat down to wait for the sun. Cold and in pain Adam Quinn stubbornly forced himself to face his future.

He had no job, and no friends now. No warm and comfortable world as a choice to be made. He had only himself. He added up his assets. He was physically strong and his injury would heal; he had a brain, now trained to read, write, and figure some. He had a trade and skill in it, and he had a few coins — no, they were only two now. And he had rage and hate and a strong will.

Again Adam recalled Kip's telling of the ruin of the Egerton business in Mount Holly and how a lawyer had brought Egerton to court for dealing in the smuggling trade. That was how he, Adam Quinn, would ruin Old Adam Jervis. He would uncover more crimes, too, and bring them all out into the open. Hadn't that evil old man been a slave trader in his youth, and his father before him? That was how the Jervis Shipping Company had gotten its start.

Adam thought of his Uncle Julian, also — a soft, weak man — and his memory held a picture of Uncle Julian watching the small boy pushed into making his cross mark without understanding what he did. Uncle Julian had looked distressed, but he had said nothing. Now Adam Jervis' grandson, as hard as the old man, would outmatch him in wits and will, and would ruin him and the whole Jervis tribe with him. Nothing could stop Adam — nothing!

Sunrise turned light snow, lying in small patches on pine needles, into a powder as pink as the lining of Tranquility's bonnet. Adam began to walk again. His swollen knee was difficult to bend, and yet the pain was not the agony of the night before. Warmth came with sunlight, touching straggling brown leaves clinging to oaks, melting fluffs of snow, softening sandy soil to the crunch of boot soles. He must find the road. If he should see Garf coming there would be time to conceal himself in the bushes.

Adam squinted at the sun, remembering that Mr. Hobson had told him to look to the sun for direction if he ever was lost in the barrens while working at ore raising. Then he hesitated. Which way was the road? Sun to the right — the road must be at his left. He turned that way, avoiding small pools where thin ice rimmed iron-brown water. As the morning advanced the sun warmed the earth and Adam, spirits rising a little, felt that perhaps luck might be turning his way. A sudden warm spell making slush of ice and causing snow to disappear was not unusual in December in south Jersey. And this was December 25. Christmas Day!

He shrugged, settling his knapsack a little easier. What of it? Christmas had never meant much to him, anyway. Joyful festivities had not been a part of his life. His immediate problem was something to eat. He had no gun for killing game and didn't know how to use one in any case. He saw little white-tailed deer gazing at him then bounding away. Birds whirred into the air as he approached, gray squirrels were not quite unafraid enough to be caught, and once he startled a gray fox into the open.

He must find a house or a settlement of some kind, if he wished to escape starvation. Adam recalled stories he had heard in Bogquake, tales of Hessian soldiers, renegades from the armies shipped here fifty years ago to conquer Continentals. When those untrained men had won the war, some of the mercenaries in the British army had disappeared into the pine barrens. There were old pineys in these forests who still spoke with a real English or a German accent — those who had, in piney talk, made "a clandestine retreat." Adam had heard, also, of some runaway slaves who had come to these forests and were still living here.

In the iron towns people called themselves pineys, and yet they said there was a great difference between them and the pineys of the deep barrens. In here there were even Quaker exiles who had taken to the jug and had been expelled from Friends Meeting.

There must be woodcutters and trappers as well as charcoalers in the pines, if he could only find them. Adam saw a road and started walking on it toward the north, or so he figured. After some time he slowed his steps, for the road was more of a trail now, at times almost disappearing altogether in underbrush. This couldn't be the main route to the Delaware River. He looked carefully and found the marks of wagon wheels, and thought he must be on a half-lost side track. Was that the sound of a creaking wagon? Crouching behind a thicket Adam watched the slow wagon pull into sight. Along with it came a smell of rotting apples. The driver dozed, chin down, hands loose on reins. Adam moved a little and a twig snapped. It sounded to him like a pistol shot.

The man lifted his head and turned toward the thicket, then apparently satisfied, he dropped his chin again. Where had Adam seen him before? Then he remembered. It was the rough-looking fellow who had cursed him and nearly run him down in Bogquake. He scarcely breathed until the wagon passed, and then he stayed where he was until no sound of it remained.

There was still the scent of apples in the air when he moved stiffly out and limped along the tracks. He realized that he was going east instead of west, for the sun was behind him. What else could he do? He hoped soon to find a road forking off to the northwest and to settlements out of the forest. Then he thought of the fishermen's towns he had heard spoken of in Bogquake. They were strung along the Atlantic Ocean coast, and there were also ports for larger vessels. What difference if he left by land or by sea?

From his arm Adam brushed a tiny beetle, sluggish in the new warmth of the thaw. He rested on a log, for he was warm enough to have beads of sweat on his upper lip and glad, at least, that he did not have to fight mosquitoes as he had done when working in the bogs.

From his left a noise came to his ears, and he began to walk quickly that way. Those must surely be the voices of children. Or was he crazily imagining things? Soon he thought he heard women chattering and calling to the children. Suddenly he caught sight of a faint trail leading through a heavy screen of underbrush and followed it. As three tumble-down shacks came into view he shouted, "Hey! Halloo there!"

He listened. Voices had ceased. Then he heard a scrambling of feet in the bushes and caught sight of ragged, wild children. They disappeared in dense tangles of vines. Adam approached slowly. He could hear birds noisy in the trees and the wind soughing in pine tops. His own feet sounded loud to him even on the needled carpet. The shacks were windowless, and their doors swung open on broken rawhide hinges. They looked like blind faces with mouths gaping.

Adam advanced slowly, disturbed and a little scared, calling out again, receiving nothing in return but silence. He looked through an open door into a bare room with

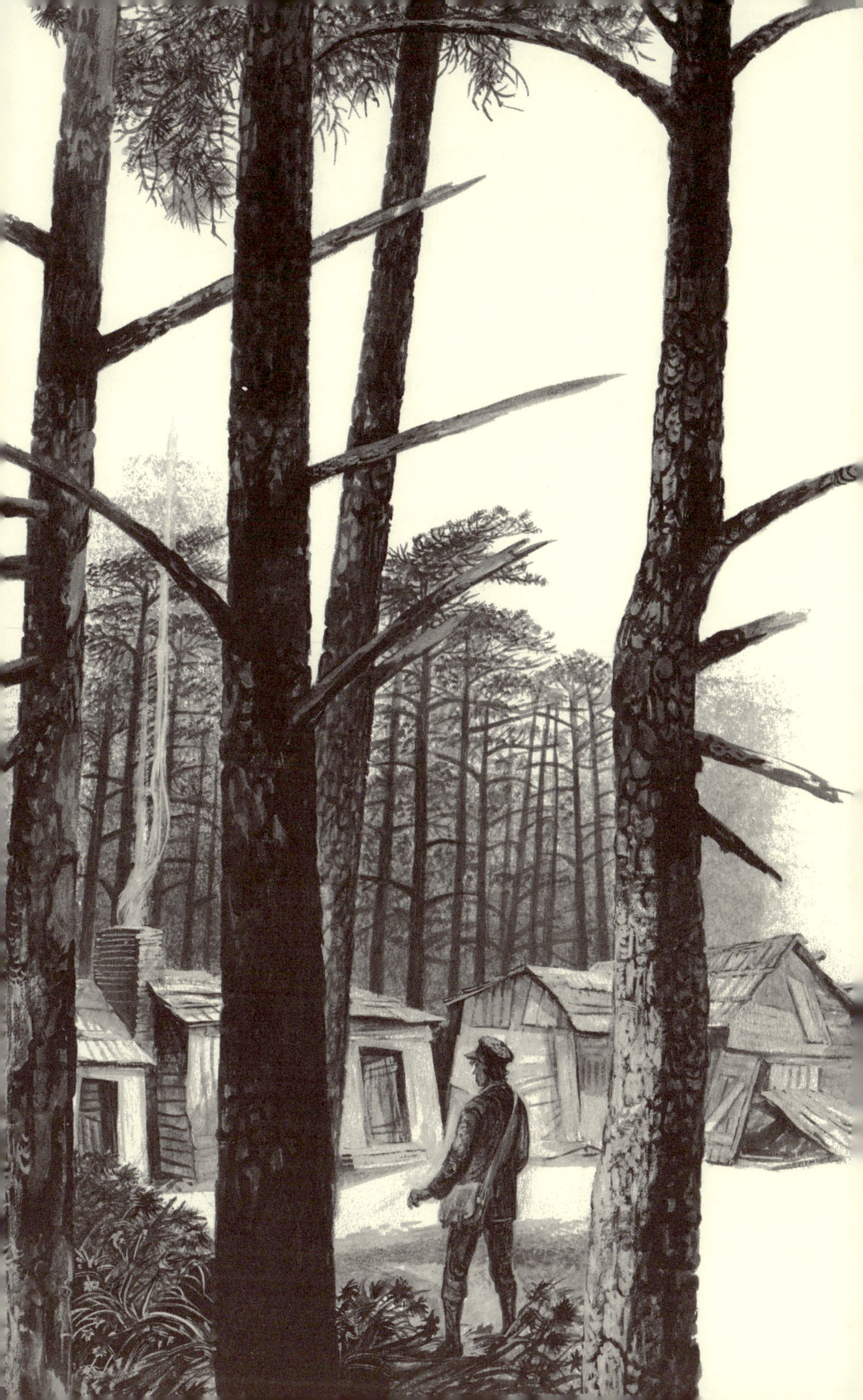

a dirt floor and no furniture. Some battered pots and kettles lay on a hearth before a mud-stick chimney, where a small wood fire burned. In the corner there were small piles of clothing, ragged blankets, and flour sacks.

He stood a few minutes, then moved slowly toward the trail. Without looking back he knew that he could get no help here. As he went he felt eyes all around him, and when he was out of sight again he heard voices of women and children.

After a time, with the sun warming the top of his head, Adam grew so thirsty that he left the tracks to look for water. He found a sluggish little run with a thin icy rim bordered with reddish mud. He stooped to drink from his hands and then walked again through dense thickets that he recognized as highbush blueberry, or huckleberry. He waded through brown ferns, crackling at his step, then stopped abruptly. Just ahead in a little forest of rustling oaks a flock of turkey buzzards flapped, screamed, and fought over the body of some furry creature. It had evidently been half eaten already by a larger predatory animal and then left to the sharp beaks and red throats of these vultures. He shuddered and found his way between tall pines, forever gossiping among themselves. Forcing himself to move on, yet he had to rest often. He thought the swelling in his knee was subsiding, although it was still bruised and stiff.

He paused and stood very still. Ahead of him was another dead animal and another flock of noisy, fighting buzzards. Adam passed around them and came to a run of brown water. There were his own footprints in the mud. He had walked in a circle. He was lost.

Dropping to the ground he tried to clear his head. He must figure out the direction of that wagon track, which had to lead somewhere. The sun — where was it? In this spot the forests of pine and oak had an undulating sameness that was almost flat. It was sandy underfoot and dry, also, for he had heard that this kind of soil never froze in winter. In what the Bogquake pineys called spongs and cripples, which were thin ice edged swampy areas, sluggish little streams meandered.

He walked slowly away from the dim ground under those trees with tangled tops and caught sight of slanting sunlight beyond a patch of weeds. It must be late afternoon, with sunset near. Chill had come down. He buttoned his flung-open jacket. There was no sight of the road.

As darkness fell Adam kept moving. He was too uneasy, and too famished with hunger, to rest. After a long time, as he circled dense thickets and moved beyond them into pines once more, he stopped again. Was that smoke he smelled? He went toward it, sniffing like a dog after a bone. Through the trees he thought he saw the flicker of a fire. Going cautiously forward, furtive now after his experience with the wild children and women, he peered into a clearing. Fire shone on a large beehive-shaped mass, where puffs of smoke issued from holes around clay sides. Behind the fire Adam could see the dim bulk of several wagons, hear horses moving restlessly, and pick out the outline of an open-sided thatched shelter. Two men stretched their legs beside the fire.

"Better give it another bucket of water or so, Josh. She's smoking too much on the off side. It's your turn."

The other man lazily got up, grasped the bail of a

bucket and doused the side where smoke was thick. "Aye, but this pit's about done. Think we can open pit and cool coal tomorrow?"

"Aye. Best move on to the east for the next pit then. Good wood there for burning, the lumber crew says."

Adam stepped forward, so relieved to find coalers, maybe from Bogquake, too, that he forget caution. A branch snapped loudly. Both men leaped to their feet, grabbing for guns. Before Adam could shout a shot exploded beside him. Another pinged to the other side. He whirled and ran with a stiff-legged gallop. Into his ears the noise of another shot plopped, so he kept going until he dropped on the earth, head pounding, breath coming in gasping sobs. There were no other sounds but late migrating whippoorwills in the laurels. And overhead a mournful *who-who-who?*

Chapter 9

He considered his position. The colliers must have thought him to be a bear, or a panther, or a pines robber. He should have called out first and not have plunged forward in the dark. Should he go back and try once more? He shivered and drew his coat close about his ears. He couldn't face those shots again. He must sleep here and return in daylight. He found as soft a spot as he could locate on the thick pine-needle carpet, drew himself up, put his head on his knapsack and slept the sleep of utter weariness. And yet somehow all night he seemed to hear whippoorwills crying — *whip-whip-poor-will* — *poor-poor* —

Plump little brown birds whirred up as Adam stood upright in sunlight, with every bone in his body aching from his cramped sleep on the ground. All about him a big flock stirred the air in a beating of wings. And then he watched the birds flying. They must be going south, those late whippoorwills.

He considered. Should he try to find that charcoal pit? He had no idea in which direction it lay. Or should he look for the road again? Yes — he was facing south and the sun was on his left hand. He decided to turn to his right and he walked with fresh hope that was soon realized when he came suddenly on thin, pale wagon tracks. This must be the main road. Or was it? It had been close by all night. Hunger was a torment in his belly. Doggedly he walked. There might be a few ripe berries even so late in the season, but he could poison himself since, except for huckleberries, he did not know one kind from another in the forest. And huckleberry bushes had long since lost their fruit.

In the distance he thought he heard a slow thud of a horse's hoofs, and then he saw an ancient nag moving toward him.

On the horse there sat an equally ancient man reading a book which rested on his saddle. Two saddlebags flapped the horse's sides with every slow jog. Adam stumbled toward the stranger. The man raised his head. The nag stopped. A wrinkled face and small, sharp eyes fixed themselves on Adam. The old man closed his book on one finger.

"And who might you be, young fellow? Well — speak up! What's your name and what are you doing out here in the wilderness? If you be a pines robber don't get any notions, for I am protected by the Lord. He gives me nothing worth stealing."

"No, sir. I'm not a thief. My name is Adam Quinn."

"Are you lost? I can scarcely see your physiognomy for all the grime and that hair in your eyes. Do you not know that John Wesley, founder of Methodism, has said that cleanliness is nigh unto godliness?"

Instead of replying to this question, severely delivered, Adam pitched forward full-length in the road. As he sat up, shaking his dizzy head to clear it, he saw the old man standing over him, his saddlebags hung on one arm.

"My boy, what ails you? You must have been felled by a swamp fever. If you but wait a moment I'll find my remedy right here somewhere in this bag. I carry only those recommended by brother Wesley."

"No, sir, I'm not sick. I'm hungry."

"Ah — not sick, but hungry — a remedy for that complaint is also at hand." The old man reached into the bag and pulled out a hard loaf and some even tougher ham.

"Eat, young man, eat hearty," and then as Adam put his teeth into the tough food the old man began to pray aloud. Adam stopped chewing and waited, but not for long, since the prayer was so short and delivered with such rapidity that he could not understand a word of it.

"Thanks, Lord," intoned the parson. "I do not believe you wish me to keep this young stranger hungry any longer."

As he ate, the preacher watched him, a smile creasing his face. He then flipped his coattails aside and, with a loud creaking of joints, sat down beside Adam in the grass. Remembering his first encounter with Kip, Adam wished him here instead of this old man, and yet he was not disposed to question his luck, either.

"You think me a Good Samaritan, brother Quinn? I am an aged Methodist long in the service of the Lord. A fisher in the lake of spiritual water. In other words — a circuit-riding parson. I believe I can claim that over the years, with the possible exception of the good doctor of the pines himself, I have covered the roads of the barrens more than any other human being. What faith do you profess, young brother?"

At a loss to reply to that question, yet too grateful for food to remain silent, Adam stood up and mumbled, "I — I scarcely know, sir — er — parson. My mother was a Quaker, and my father a Catholic, but they are both dead now."

"Ah, then you are a heathen, sprung from two kinds of heretic stock, and a brand for the burning. That is worse than no faith at all." His voice rose in a singsong, dry as winter oak leaves, and yet with a power and a strength that carried far up and down the empty road. "You may yet be saved, brother. Will you journey along with me? I can offer you a ride from time to time, for I see that your leg be stiffened. You stand on one foot like a crane in a bog. Unless that be your choice of position to comfort you? I am accustomed to footing it now and then."

Adam declined, politely but firmly. The parson was traveling south to Bogquake, and Adam was going north, he hoped. To seek work he said.

"North? You can't go north that way. This road comes from the coast, where I have been this last month. You needs must follow it one way or another, east or west, since there be no other road hereabouts."

And so with a solemn nod and murmured blessings in his singsong voice, the aged Methodist got onto his horse with a surprising agility, given him by long practice, placed his book open and, clucking to his horse, he rode slowly away, leaving the pace to his steed. But as Adam stepped out in the opposite direction he heard a shout, "Young fellow, you watch out! I am clothed in the armor of Jehovah. Not you, young man! There be pines robbers in the wilderness. There be murderers."

His last words rang in Adam's ears as he trudged the road. "Murderers!" He spoke of me and didn't know it, thought Adam, for I am a murderer. What does it matter if I did not mean to kill? A wave of shame flooded over him as he realized that for weeks he had not thought of his guilt. Misery settled down on him like a sullen thunderhead.

When he had covered a mile or more he stopped for a drink. As he leaned over the stream he heard a snort just behind him and jerked to his feet to face the fierce red eyes of a wild hog. Adam fled as fast as his limping leg would allow. When he stopped at last to get a breath to ease his bursting chest, he listened and heard nothing but his own gasps — and the wind forever sighing in the treetops. He looked around. There was no sign of the wild boar, and no sign of the road.

After a rest on a log Adam turned and started back in the direction from which he had come. He did not know how long he wandered, or whether he walked in a circle once more. Nothing recognizable appeared. He could no longer use the sun for guide, as it had vanished behind the pines. A cold wind was rising, and when he looked up he saw the sky moving rapidly in a swollen mass of cloud.

Once he thought he saw a tiny light near the ground, moving forward in the distance, and stumbled after it. His feet sank in swamp mud, so he hurriedly turned another way. Some bogs held quicksand in their depths, and Mr. Hobson had told him never to go into a bog after dark. Perhaps that light was the awful will-o'-the-wisp he remembered dimly from an Irish tale told him by his father. Perhaps the beckoning glow was luring him to his death. Who would ever know or care what happened to Adam Quinn? He gave his shoulders a stubborn shake under his father's knapsack and said aloud, "Stop feeling sorry for yourself! You care. That's enough."

Soon it was too dark to see clouds moving overhead, but he continued to walk slowly, arms stretched out before him to ward off branches and tell him of thickets. His feet searched out the earth, feeling pine needles. He avoided sound of water. Once he froze as a wild animal odor swept over him. Was it a bear nearby, or a wild boar, or only a polecat? A soft sound, and the odor disappeared.

Just before dawn he felt sand crunching underfoot and the wind rising in his face. He seemed to be walking in thick undergrowth which scratched and grabbed at his legs, making it difficult to advance. Now and then lightning zigzagged down and showed him an eerie sight. As far as he could see in the flash there was a vast plain covered with dwarf trees with tortured limbs. Their tops came only to his waist or shoulder. Trapped, Adam stood where he had halted. He shivered violently as a nighthawk plummeted close before his eyes, wings zooming in his ears. Wind died, and rain beat down. It pounded and stung his face.

As suddenly as it had come the storm swept out to sea.

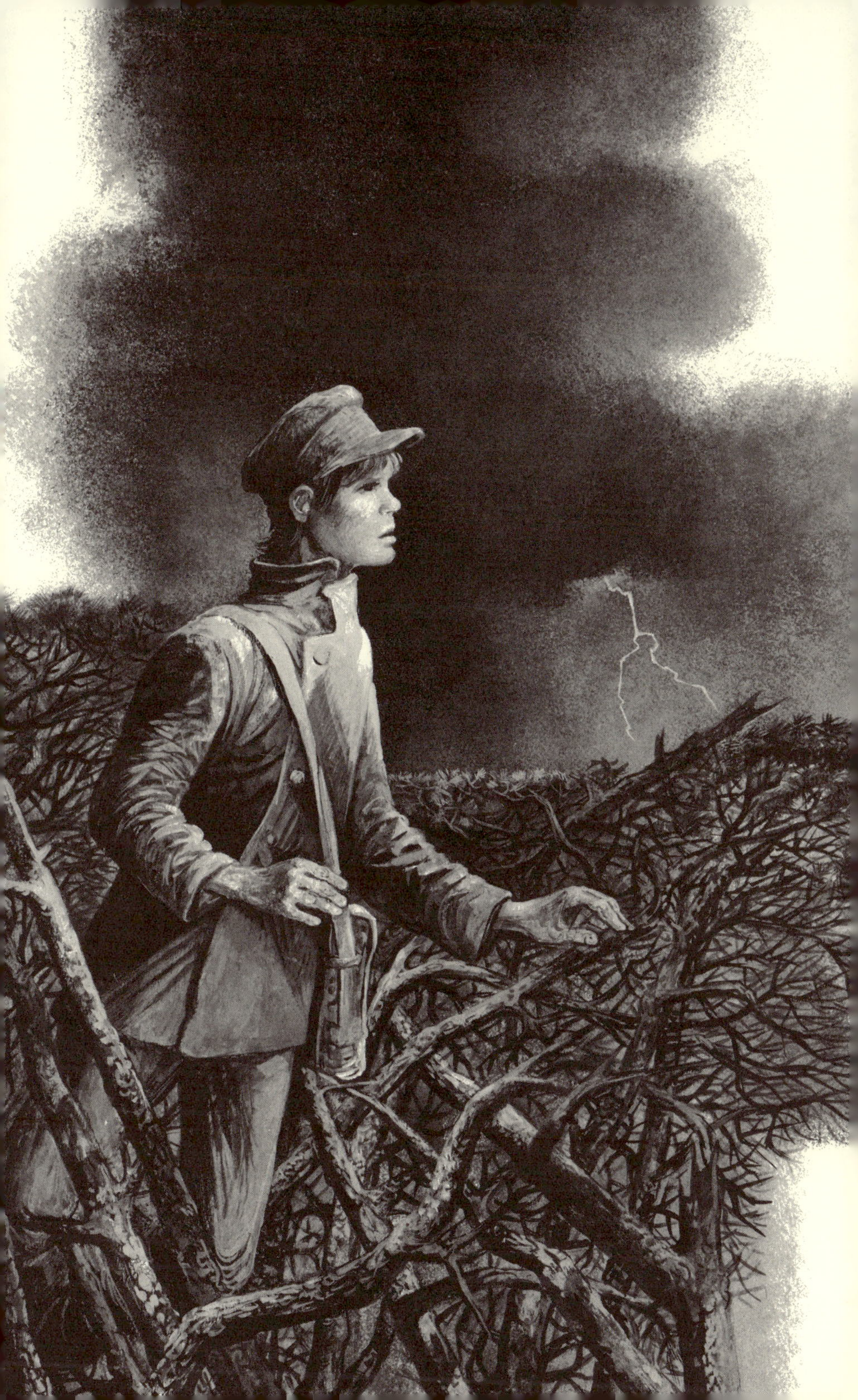

Adam did not move until a sun on fire glared angry on his right. A covey of gray heath hens flew up. Overhead the black and white wings of a fish hawk circled and turned and disappeared toward the ocean. Adam's cramped knees loosened, his shoulders drooped, and his eyes stared at thousands of stunted oak and pine tops. He was a giant in a land of pygmies.

At last he saw a small hill rising to his left beyond this strange forest. What was there to do but start that way? He began to push stubbornly through the queer little trees, gradually making his way across the plains. Startled birds rose and small white-tailed bucks and does leaped over the treetops before him. Near noon, sun hot on his head, he came to the end of the plains and began to climb the hill. It was a relief to see oaks, an occasional buttonwood, sweet bays, junipers, and other tall trees whose names he didn't know. At the top of the hill he stared down in first one direction and then another.

There was no sign of settlement or of house, or of road. And yet — was that a wisp of smoke curling above the pines? He closed his eyes, then looked again. It was far beyond the dwarf forest in the high trees, but not so far he could not find it soon. Forgetting his weariness he struggled through the edge of this grotesque plain and came out at last into sweet pine woods.

Recovering caution as he approached what he judged to be a camp, and remembering his experience with the colliers, Adam moved quietly until he reached a clump of holly. He saw a shack where someone must be living, since there was a low burning fire in the center of a cleared space, a kettle hanging over the fire, and a second fire behind it with a copper tank and a coil of pipe over it. A strong smell of fermenting fruit hung over the clearing.

A wagonload of rotting apples stood nearby, and piled on the ground not far away was an array of earthen jugs, wooden casks, and a few glass bottles. His eyes swept over these and came to rest on an old woman who emerged from the shack and came to the fire to bend over the kettle. There was no one else in sight.

He considered carefully. Should he take a chance of running into that dangerous-looking man whose wagon that must be? A woman would not be so risky to face. He must get food and help in finding the road. He didn't want to frighten her, so he walked slowly from behind the bush with his hands held high. The woman raised her head, reached down, and came up with a musket. Adam stopped in his tracks, arms sinking to his sides.

"I've got a bead on you. Put your hands back up and come here slow and easy-like."

Chapter 10

"All right. Come closer."

He advanced slowly, arms up.

"That's far enough. What you doin' here?"

"I'm lost. Looking for the road."

"Nobody comes this deep in the barrens hereabouts but us Scarfys." She studied him with sharp eyes. "You runnin' from the law?"

"Aye, ma'am."

"All right then — I best hold you till my boys come back. I'll feed you, but don't get any notions of runnin'."

As Adam ate the stew she ladled into a pan for him the old woman kept her eyes on him suspiciously.

"Where you from? You a runaway redemptioner?"

"No, ma'am. Apprentice."

"Hum. You found our camp. How do I know you ain't lying and figure to inform on us to the sheriff of Tallytown?"

"No. I'm running from a constable myself."

"You ain't no piney. You talk city-like. You from Philadelphy?"

Adam nodded. They could hear sound of wagon wheels jolting over the ground. A whoop from two men, one after the other, gave notice of arrival as they came into the clearing.

"Gorramighty, Ma, who you got there?"

"I bagged a runaway 'prentice, Bo. Lost, he says."

The bearded man scowled at Adam, and the other, who was close to Adam in age, stared with mean eyes and mouth open as if he had very little sense. The older brother shouted, "Rudd, tie him up and set him against the shack. Hands'll do. Ma will drop him if he tries to run."

The younger fellow grabbed Adam's knapsack and rummaged through it. He took the two coins, bit each with strong yellow teeth, found them to be silver, and threw the knapsack on the ground. Then he tied Adam's hands behind his back and shoved him against the shack.

Another whoop sent birds skittering as a hunter came in with a deer carcass slung over his shoulders. This man was the ruffian whom Adam had seen twice before. Now he seemed less dangerous than either of the other brothers. A dog, shaggy and caked with mud and with one leg missing, slunk from the trees and crept up beside Adam. It was easy to tell that the beast was used to cruelty and saw compassion in this stranger's eyes.

The men stretched out around the fire near the old

woman, who sat with puffing corncob pipe. Disconnected talk came to Adam, sometimes plain and sometimes too low to hear clearly.

"Get some fire sticks, Rudd."

The young Scarfy pulled himself to his feet and threw more wood on the blaze. Then he moved slowly toward Adam, eyes gleaming in the firelight, mouth open in a grin. Suddenly he grasped the handle of a bowie knife in his belt and stepped back with one foot. Plunk! Adam flinched and braced himself against the wall. The knife quivered beside his ear. The dog fled for the woods. Rudd laughed, withdrew the knife, and moved back. Adam held his breath, face white.

"Rudd! Rudd! You quit that now. Ain't I told you to stop that kind of playing. Come over here."

"Aw, Ma, let me have some fun, can't you?"

But he moved obediently away and threw himself down, grumbling loudly.

"Bo, did you get that load of rum downa shore? Where be it? I didn't hear you driving it in."

"They run us off, Ma. They got two men with shotguns riding on them rum wagons now. We ain't taken no smugglers' rum for a long spell. You know that. But I got a new plan — listen to this —"

Voices were lowered, then raised again. "Didn't get much for the lightning in Bogquake, Ma, but I picked up that load of fruit for nothing at Lute's farm. Now looka here, Ma — I told you I got a scheme for tomorrow."

In extreme fatigue Adam was finding it hard to stay awake. He shook his head to clear it as he listened. He had missed some of what they said and couldn't puzzle out the next talk: "Can't wait — well, he's coming along the road tomorrow on his way home. Got a route regular as clockwork, he has. How do I know? Folks in Tallytown talk about him, and I heard at the jug tavern he's got a cache of gold pieces sewed in his coattails."

"What you doing in that tavern, Bo? You want to be taken by the sheriff?"

"He ain't got proof of nothing, Ma. Let him catch us with the goods or find this camp, and he can take us in. But he won't."

"I don't like it. What about that doctor?"

"We can get more out of that doctor than just his gold, Ma. If we can jump him on the road tomorrow morning, hide him out here — worth more — downriver — good prices —"

This made no sense at all to Adam, who was looking longingly at the dark woods and considering making a run for it, although he knew that the old woman would shoot him instantly. Bo and Will got up and came toward Adam. They grasped him roughly, pulled him to his feet and took him to the back of the shack where they shoved him into a lean-to shed and drew the bolt on the outside of the door.

In darkness Adam sat leaning against a barrel, with the rope around his wrists dangling behind him. He heard the Scarfys moving into the shack and then a series of snores. Far away some night creature gave a strange, monotonous cry.

When his eyes grew accustomed to the darkness he could make out bottles, jugs, and barrels, and the air was heavy with odors of rum and applejack. A thin sliver of moonlight crept between boards in the wall of the lean-to. He got to his knees and moved that way. Then he turned his back, took hold of the lower board under the crack with his bound hands, and pulled hard. The rusty nails gave way with a noise that to him was a cannon blast. Pain shot up his arms. He paused, holding his breath, and heard nothing but snores.

His fingers explored the planks below the broken board and found them crumbling with rot, and he slowly tore them apart and opened a hole large enough for his body. Then he wormed through and stood up in the clearing, gingerly making his way to the dark forest. As he went he thought he had heard something behind him. He stopped and turned. He could see nothing. The cooking fire was dying, but the one under the bubbling still flamed high. One of the Scarfys would come to build the still fire up before long. Adam moved faster into the trees.

Again he thought he had heard something. He turned quickly and saw a low shadow outlined in moonlight. It was poised motionless behind him. Adam whispered urgently, "Dog, come!"

The animal crept toward him until its eyes gleamed up sadly. Together they quickened their pace, less concerned about the noise they made now that the glow of the clearing and scent of cooking apple mash had disappeared. In the distance, just on the edge of the clearing, they could still hear, now and then, the horses moving on their tethers. Taking stock of the position of the moon Adam tried to figure in which direction he should go. He knew there would be no wagon tracks visible on these pine needles, even if the light allowed him to see. He located a thicket and dropped on the ground behind it, burrowing into it as much as possible as he waited for dawn. A wide tree trunk made a rest for his back, but he could not sleep. No more could the dog as it lay with muscles tensed beside him. Once Adam murmured, "I wish you could untie my hands, dog. How can I persuade you to chew this rope loose?" The dog raised its melancholy eyes, then dropped muzzle to paws. There came that lonely night sound again, poignant, far away. Adam shivered. It must be the cry of a bird, and yet it sounded like the sobbing wail of a lost child.

He spent the remainder of the night trying desperately to loosen the rope that bound his wrists. Leaning forward, turning his hands, twisting, attempting to catch the knot with fingers stiffened by cold in a new and bitter wind. Now and then he got up to walk about, stumbling over roots, trying to warm his feet. Then he sat again, the dog beside him. As he leaned against the tall white cedar, trying to work his hands free, the night seemed endless to him. And then, at last, with wrists skinned raw, he felt the rope growing looser. Biting his lips until he tasted blood Adam managed to grasp the loop with his right fingers and slowly pushed it back through the knot. He was free!

Rubbing his wrists he became aware that dawn was about to break, so, getting to his feet, he picked up the rope, coiled it tightly, and thrust it into his belt. No use throwing anything away. This must be the Quaker coming out in him, he thought grimly, for caution and frugality had certainly not been part of his father's character. He felt around for his cap, then remembered that it had been left, along with his knapsack, in that clearing. So he pulled his collar high about reddened ears and began to walk, following the direction he thought the wagon must have come. The dog loped behind his heels in its peculiar three-legged motion.

With a foot about to come down, Adam stopped short. Swiftly he dropped to the ground and crawled into a stinging holly bush. The dog dodged under and pressed tightly against him. Bo and Rudd came into view through the leaves, swinging along with the slow, steady pace of woodsmen, and Adam caught a glint of early sunshine on pistols and knife sheaths in their belts. After they had passed, the fugitives followed at a safe distance. When they came to wagon tracks Adam decided to bear away to his right, for he thought he could now locate the road farther along beyond the point the two Scarfys seemed to be making for. He was risking losing himself again, but he must chance that. The sun found the boy and dog moving as rapidly as possible around thickets and bogs to clearer pinelands. Adam was confident that he would soon find the road.

There it was! He dropped down to rest and the dog stretched out nearby. After a little while they got to their weary feet again and moved northward on the road. The dog stopped, ears back. Adam listened. He heard voices somewhere ahead where the road made a turn. Those must be the Scarfys. Bo and Rudd must have intercepted that doctor farther north than Adam had thought — or he himself had walked in a half circle. He must have a weapon. Adam left the road and found a stout stick. With this in hand he and the shivering dog crept forward behind shielding thickets, until they could see, just around the bend of the road, a buggy standing behind an old horse.

Bo and the doctor must be on the other side of the buggy, out of sight. Rudd was hauling a large leather case from the box behind the seat.

"Gorramighty! Gimme that coat!" From out of sight came the sound of ripping and a yell of rage. "There ain't no gold pieces in his coattails!"

Rudd had placed his pistol carelessly on the edge of the buggy box and was leaning over the case, tossing out medicines and bandages behind him.

Fury took Adam. He rose, clutching the cudgel with both hands, and leaped into the road. With a wide swing he swept the pistol into the weeds. Rudd straightened up just as the stick swung again and struck his legs below the knee. He fell backward with a hoarse cry that ended abruptly. Adam flung himself at the pistol, then jumped around the buggy.

He saw Bo holding the ripped coat of the doctor, who stood with a hand on his horse's bridle.

"Don't you move!" shouted Adam. "And drop that gun!"

Bo let go of coat and pistol. Then Adam turned his eyes to the doctor, seeing with amazement that he was a black man.

"Get — get that gun, sir — if you can."

The Negro man in dark trousers and white shirt quietly took the pistol from the road and held it steadily trained on Bo Scarfy. Adam grabbed Bo's bowie knife from his belt and jerked the rope from his own. As he knotted it tightly around Scarfy wrists he heard the doctor saying, "Young chap, you saved my life, or my freedom. I don't know rightly which. Maybe both. I thank you for it. You must have killed that other one behind the buggy. He's powerful quiet."

Abruptly Adam's rage receded. He was appalled as the thought rushed over him that he might have another lifeless victim to remember. It was no crime to strike down a robber, yet he did not want to take the life of any man again. He felt cold sweat trickling down his back.

"I hit at his legs — I — I couldn't have killed him."

"I'll take a look. First we had better tie this rascal to a tree."

They found one not too big in girth to accommodate the length of the rope and left the bearded man sitting on the ground cursing. Adam held back at the sight of Rudd's blood as the doctor swiftly pulled off the man's boots and slit his trouser legs. He felt Rudd's pulse and lifted his eyelids to peer into them. Then he turned. "He's unconscious, must have struck his head on the wheel as he fell. But he's not dead. See — he's coming to now. He'll live to hang yet."

Getting to his feet somewhat stiffly the doctor gathered up vials and bottles, threw broken glass into the bushes, and placed undamaged medicines back in the chest. Adam set himself to helping gather up things from the road. The doctor found his clean flour sack bandages, poured a pungent liquid on them, put a wad of moss inside, and bound up Rudd Scarfy's leg with a flat strip of wood taken from a supply in the chest.

Rudd's eyes opened. The doctor said, "You will be all right. After a time, that is. Can you sit up?"

Rudd struggled to a sitting position, making hoarse noises in his throat, and the doctor said calmly, "His right leg is broken. He won't use it for a while. Help me put him over by the other bandit."

Adam hoisted Rudd by his shoulders, and, with the doctor taking his legs carefully, they got him sitting against a tree. The brothers were cursing in such a foul duet that the doctor said to Adam, with a smile, "Suppose we take leave of these two gentlemen before they make us deaf. Get into my buggy, young fellow. If you're going my way?"

"What will happen to them?"

"We be fairly close to Tallytown here. I'll send the sheriff out for them. No danger of their going anywheres." He turned to look curiously at his companion. "Where you dropped from so suddenlike I can't figure."

Adam sank back against the cracked leather cushion and tried not to think how disreputable and like a pines robber he himself appeared. He took a better look at this tall, black man with his cap of gray hair and calm face. Joined with the clop of the horse's hoofs there seemed to be another sound, faint and yet distinct. Adam twisted about and caught sight of a mongrel loping along, tongue out, body jouncing from side to side on three legs.

"What's that?" The doctor drew in his reins and stopped. Staring over his shoulder he exclaimed, "By Beelzebub and all his imps — what is that following us?"

"The Scarfy dog. He took up with me last night. He wouldn't hurt anybody. He's scared of everything."

"You want to take him along?"

Adam paused to think. He didn't need a dog with him, not with what he had to do, and certainly not that peculiarly ugly specimen. And yet he said slowly, "Aye. I do."

"Very well, then. Call him. If he's going with us he might as well ride, especially since he seems to have lost a leg somewhere."

Adam jumped down and waited until the dog was eagerly licking his hands. Then he lifted him into the buggy, where he pushed him against his feet.

"Now, where did you say you came from?"

"It's a long story, sir. I saw those pineys going after you and crept up on them in the underbrush."

"I be a piney myself, but there's two kinds in these woods. How did you perform the miracle of producing that rope? I've seen many an astonishing thing, but never anything more so than the way you lit on that man and then whipped out a rope to secure the other one. Do you go about the highways equipped for tying up robbers?"

Adam laughed, "Well, scarcely so. The Scarfys had me tied with that same piece of rope last night in their camp. I wandered in there by accident looking for help. I was lost in the barrens. I got away last night."

"Lucky for you that you did. Scarfys are long wanted by the sheriff, murdering critters that they be, but they slither away like pines snakes every time." The doctor eased himself more comfortably into the seat groove that had worn to fit him. "Will you give me your name, young man? If you wish? I don't require it."

"Adam Quinn. I'm heading north to look for work in the blacksmith trade."

"Then Adam Quinn, you will ride with me to my home and stay the night, I hope. My wife will not be able to do enough for someone who rescued me from robbers. Or could be slave runners? Some will sell a black man into slavery be he a free man or not. Slave stealing is done outside the law here in New Jersey, that we all know, though Jersey has a law against slavery. My home is a few miles beyond Tallytown on the Fork-ed Road. First we must see Mr. Bollock, the sheriff, for he will be much in your debt if you can tell him how to reach that hidden camp. The Scarfys' moonshine still is well enough known hereabouts, but never yet located. Bollock has not been able to catch them red-handed so he could make his arrest, even though they come openly into Tallytown sometimes."

Adam's eyes grew wary, and he said slowly, "Well, sir — maybe —"

The doctor cut his eyes sharply toward Adam, then looked away as he said, "My name is Jenkens. I'm pleased to make your acquaintance, and that's the truth. I'm the only doctor in all the deep pine barrens, I reckon, except in the towns. They call me Dr. Micah."

Before he thought Adam exclaimed, "Aye — I've heard of you in Bogquake." He didn't add that he had not heard that Dr. Micah was a Negro. Once Mrs. Hobson had spoken of the doctor of the pines, but Adam could not remember much of what she had said.

"Ah, in Bogquake. I seldom get that far, but do go there once in a while. They have a licensed doctor in Bogquake, Wellfleet by name, who thinks little enough of such as I be. You come from Bogquake?"

"Aye. But from Philadelphia before that."

"Thought you be city wise, somehow, from your talk. Well, Adam, we are coming to Tallytown now."

Adam said nothing more as they rode along the short street and drew up in the middle of the one block which was the center of the village. The sheriff's office and one-room jail was sandwiched between a small hole-in-the-wall jug tavern and the store. Adam jumped out of the buggy as it stopped, followed instantly by the dog. Clenching and unclenching his fists, he burst out, "I thankee for the ride. I'll say farewell now."

With that he strode off around the corner, where he halted to listen, face red with shame at his rudeness. For a long moment he heard nothing. Then came the creak of the buggy. A door slammed. Adam went along behind houses, through some fields and woods, and came out on the road farther on. The dog kept pace with the boy, whose stride became slower and more weary as he walked.

Chapter 11

A<small>LTHOUGH HE WALKED STEADILY</small> it was not long before he felt a need to rest. He sat on a log and looked at the sores on the dog's back as the unhappy animal stretched out nearby. Adam thought that his own spirit was festering too. What would it matter if he and this pathetic creature perished together right there? Yet he knew he would not give up, no matter how low he felt.

He was trying to push aside the thought that he had injured another man; he did not like to remember the blind fury with which he had struck Rudd Scarfy. He was not sorry to have rescued the doctor, but he wished that he could have done so without dealing that blow. He was aware of the sound of wheels, and the dog rose and growled low in his throat, then slunk behind Adam.

A shabby buggy drew up beside them and Dr. Micah called out, "Get in, Adam, and bring the ugly beast with you. I live beyond the next fork at the crossroad, and it's only a whoop and a holler to here. Bess will be mighty glad to welcome you for the night. You look right well tuckered out, boy."

Boy and dog got into the buggy and, head turned away, Adam muttered, "I'm sorry I had to leave like that. But I figured seeing the sheriff would take more time than I've got."

The doctor gave him a quick glance, but said nothing, except "Gee up, Lafayette, we want to go home."

After a little Adam asked hesitantly, "Dr. Jenkens, did you — did you tell the sheriff about me?"

"Why, no, not any particulars. He was out, you see, so I left a message. I just said that two of the Scarfys were tied up waiting for him by the roadside about nine miles south on the road, and Mr. Bollock could go fetch them. I said they attacked me and a stranger helped me. You want me not to say it was you, I sort of guessed that."

"Aye." Adam unclenched the fist resting on his knee, then yanked on the lock of hair falling over one eye.

The doctor smiled suddenly. "All right. You helped me. I'll help you."

Adam said slowly, "Dr. Micah, I didn't mean to hit that man that hard. I'm powerful glad he's not dead. Even if he is vicious — I don't ever want to kill —"

"You don't know your own strength, boy, do you?"

As the carriage turned into the barnyard he added, "Well, now, Adam Quinn, I reckon you've got a real hot temper. So, if that be the case, you have to learn to leash it up. Why do I sermonize you, boy? You saved my life with that mighty blow. Anyway, Scarfy's leg will heal, and he will have a-plenty time in jail where he ain't got no place to walk, anyway. No place at all." He chuckled as he got out of the buggy.

"Come inside and meet Bess, the boss woman of the Jenkens house."

Adam had seen Negroes before, of course, in Philadelphia, but he had not really known them. In fact, he had not ever thought about slavery at all, taking it for granted as a fact of life outside New Jersey, until Tranquility had talked of it to him, and he had read John Woolman's *Journal*. He had baited her temper with questions about the "black corner" in Friends Meeting just to rile her a bit. Free black men and women of Bogquake lived in a small group at Sandy Run, a half mile or so from the furnace works. He had labored in the bogs beside some of these men, but he had not been talking much to anybody then, black or white. Nevertheless, his own consciousness of enforced servitude had made him aware, in his present hunted condition, of what slavery might mean. Suddenly he realized that he liked Dr. Jenkens, and as he stepped inside and was greeted by Mrs. Jenkens he liked her, too.

She was a plump, motherly, brown woman with big expressive eyes. They snapped angrily as she heard her husband telling of the fight on the road.

"Oh, the Lord be praised for preserving me my man. I thank you, Adam Quinn." Then, whirling about with astonishing agility, she exclaimed, "I told you, Micah Jenkens, you would be set on sooner or later, traveling along the lonesome roads. The last time you went downa shore I warned you to carry a gun. Didn't I tell you, now? Now, didn't I?"

"Bess, you did tell me. About a hundred times, as I recollect. But what can I do? I must make my rounds, and my rounds take me along roads through the lonesome barrens. I couldn't shoot that pistol you got for me, anyway. I trust in the Lord to protect me, and he did. With Adam."

She went to the stove and dished up enough food for six young men, each as tall and as big as Adam.

"Sit down. Lord, am I going to feed you!"

Micah laughed at their guest's confusion. "Bess, don't you scare this young fellow to an early grave with your thankfulness. Sit down. Our house is yours."

Adam wondered how Mrs. Jenkens knew that she would need extra food for a stranger, and it was later that he understood that she was always prepared to feed anybody who came, as many did come every day in the year.

Suddenly he remembered that dog. It had held back suspiciously as they had gone indoors. Adam went out and called.

"Dog! Come."

No sign of it. He whistled. From behind the rain barrel near the back door, the dog crept over to him, putting out a tongue to lick his hand.

"My Lord a-mercy," shouted Mrs. Jenkens in the doorway. "What is that critter?"

"My dog," grinned Adam. "He's hungry, I reckon."

"Your dog? Looks like Satan's own limb to me. Will he bite?"

The two farm dogs, catching strange scent, came dashing out of the barn at the mongrel, which slunk rapidly under the porch. Mrs. Jenkens made a rush at her dogs and chased them away.

"That ugly varmint belies his looks, that he do. Bring him inside, Adam."

Adam whistled again, and the dog followed him into the kitchen, then moved over to the hearth and crouched down in the edge of warm ashes. Mrs. Jenkens brought a pan of food and another of water. They watched the dog until every scrap of food had disappeared and water was being loudly slurped. Then she said, shaking her head, "I hate to touch that critter. It's got as many sores and sorrows as Job himself, a-sitting there in the ashes. I'll call it Job, since you seem not to have a name for it."

She moved away and returned with a pan of warm water, salves, and a healing powder, with which she treated the dog's sores. Job made not a sound or a move, and when she had finished she patted him gingerly on his shaggy head, saying, "Tell you one thing, you got to scrub him tomorrow, Adam. He's the foulest smelling beast my nose ever tackled."

Crossroads House was an old building made of weather-blackened cedar slabs. Once it had been an inn, Adam was told, and the doctor had bought it for almost nothing after it had been abandoned. He and his wife had made it into an office, a home, and a place of refuge for any sick man, woman, or child who came. Dr. Micah walked with his slow, loose-limbed stride about his domain as he showed Adam the place. In one room bottles of all shapes and colors were stacked — wide-mouthed and narrow — some with bubbles thick in Jersey glass, others of plain window glass — long-necked, or squat. They were mixed with earthenware crocks, brown and gray, large and small.

"You wonder how I got so many of such different kinds?" asked the doctor with some pride. "I scrounge 'em from dumps and trash piles. I collect old patent medicine bottles from apothecary shops. I take in all unbroken rum and whiskey bottles once filled by Mr. Booz, the distiller of Philadelphia."

Adam looked up at a rustling sound overhead, not unlike dry wintry leaves clinging to an oak in the forest. He saw bunches of plants swinging back and forth in a chilly draft entering between open cracks in the walls of this ancient inn.

"Must get time to plug up those holes," muttered the herb doctor, frowning. "Old mud daubing keeps peeling out between the slabs."

The next room had two fireplaces and must once have been the kitchen where Continental soldiers warmed their legs and lifted tankards of hot wine, or West Indian rum, before going out to battle troopers sent to these shores by King George. Each hearth was very much in use, but not in the way intended by the builders. Blackened pot-bellied kettles swung on cranes over the flames, filling the room with sharp odors of simmering herbs. The hearths were crowded with pans and pots bringing such a mixture of smells to Adam's nose that he coughed with watering eyes. Bess Jenkens' own kitchen made a strange partnership with the herbs, and yet through some alchemy of her own she managed to do her cooking without bringing noxious brews to her table.

They walked through a storeroom crowded with sacks of coarse brown sugar for medicinal syrups and a small room where mortars and pestles were jumbled on a table among piles of dried roots. On one side homemade chests of drawers were labeled with the unpronounceable names of healing plants.

"My mother was Indian, you know," said Dr. Micah. "She was one of the last Delawares in this part of the state. She lived on the first Indian reservation in the nation, over yonder toward Coopers' Landing, before she married. Indian Mills it's called now, though it's only a crossroads, and no Leni-Lenapes are there anymore. All that survive are in the west, pushed beyond the Pennsylvania mountains."

So that was why the doctor did not look much like the other Negroes Adam had seen, not even like his wife. Except for his darker color and his short, tight cap of gray hair, he might have been one of the hawk-nosed, high-cheekboned people of the forests.

Micah seemed to enjoy talking to Adam. "My father was a slave in the Edwards family in Bogquake." He smiled at Adam's surprise. "He was set free by old Mr. Simon Edwards, father of the present ironmaster. Some folks thought then that only Quakers didn't believe in slavery, as that was before the law against it was passed in Jersey, but Methodist Simon Edwards freed all of his young slaves soon as they married, and gave them jobs in his ironworks. Bishop Asbury himself had converted Simon Edwards on one of the bishop's peregrinating rides through the piny woods at the turn of the century, and from then on a better Methodist there never was. What church faith do you profess, Adam?"

"I don't rightly know, Dr. Micah." He caught his lower lip between his teeth before saying, "I guess not any. My father was Roman and my mother Quaker, but I was parted from them and can scarcely remember them. I never took to the shouting of my master's wife in her church, when she forced me to go there."

"There be all kinds of faith, and all kinds of folks in them, and some follow the faith that dwells in the wind in the trees and the waters flowing to the sea."

The doctor moved into another room, where he showed Adam benches for patients to wait. Upstairs were rooms, plain, bare, and clean, each with a home-built plank bed and straw-filled mattress; each had snowy bleached feedsacks spread out. Each had a pile of quilts, much patched but warm, at the foot.

"All these rooms," wondered Adam. "Do you have many visitors?"

"A many we do have. They come. We never know when, sometimes not know where from, and if they be very sick we bed them down for a while. Right now our last one left us yesterday. Sometimes all beds are filled and keeps Bess and me a-hopping."

He added, "You are tuckered, boy. Go to bed. Take the first room to your left."

Adam heard him going down the creaky old stair boards. Job waited solemnly while Adam washed from the copper jug and basin of hot water left for him by Mrs. Jenkens, and leaped onto the bed at his master's feet as Adam dropped there, fully clothed, and pulled the quilts about his chin. Sometime later he heard steps ascending, low voices, the doctor's measured tread, and a sound of front door slamming. Then, as wintry wind howled about the eaves of Crossroads House, he slept as he had not done for a long time.

Next morning was bitter cold, in the sudden coming and going of weather in down Jersey. Adam shivered as he descended the stairs, seeing snow stuck in fluffs and ragged puffs against the barnyard fence beyond green glass of windowlights. The whole house rattled and complained. Mrs. Jenkens dodged about stuffing rags into chinks, voice raised.

"I told you, Micah Jenkens, if you didn't daub those cracks before winter you going to be sorry. That wind will freeze our bones solid."

"Bess, bones be solid without freezing," chuckled Micah, who seemed vastly amused at his wife's complaints, his arm moving in a steady, circular motion as he ground herbs with a pestle in a stone mortar.

Adam went over and took a rag from her hands. "Good day, Mistress Jenkens. I'll stuff the cracks. You do what you have to do. Where do I find more rags?"

"More rags? Rags is short supply here all the time, though folks do bring them in to us often as they can. Well, Adam, if need be and you can't find more in the storeplace yonder where sugar sacks are kept, then rip up your shirttail. If you got one. Maybe you ain't. We've got to keep that wind out somehow."

She moved off laughing, calling back to him, "When you're done, come in the kitchen and eat."

On his way into the kitchen Adam drew in a deep breath of hot corn cake and frying bacon. He felt rested for the first time since leaving Bogquake, and in the tingling cold he thought he could heave mountains about if called upon to do so. Mrs. Jenkens was rushing around talking, laughing, shouting complaints, and Adam could hear the door slamming once, twice, with the doctor's slow voice calm as the eye of a hurricane.

At last Mrs. Jenkens flung herself into a chair, wiping

her brow with her apron in spite of the cold. "Adam, a busy place this you've fallen into. And if you're heading for the city just to look for work, why not stay here with us for a little spell?" Her face took on a concerned look, "My man does too much. He needs some help. He's well past seventy now, you know."

"I'm not a doctor, Mistress Jenkens, so how could I work here?"

Quietly, a little anxiety showing, she spoke in a different voice. "Micah ain't a doctor either, Adam. He wanted to be — oh, all his born days he wanted to be a real physician. Ever since he watched old Dr. Bolton curing folks in Bogquake, when Micah was a skinny tadpole. That doctor brought him back to life when he came down with a fever and nearly heard the flap of angels' wings. Another time a wagonload of green lumber fell on Micah — just missed crushing him. The old doctor set both Micah's legs, and from that time Micah's thought of nothing but curing people."

"He isn't a doctor?"

"No. How could a black man ever get medical schooling? Even before the license law came in. Nowadays you get hauled off to the jailhouse if you do doctoring without your papers. To get a paper signed and sealed you have to have training in Philadelphia Medical School, or some other, or certified by working years long with a physician."

"Then how can he practice medicine without getting arrested?"

"Well, Micah's got a good friend who's a judge in Mount Holly. He told him if he only takes money for his medicines, not for treating folks, he's all right with the law. So that's what he does."

"Then you don't get paid for looking after sick people?"

"No, that we don't. We sell herb teas, brews, infusions, pills, powders, and syrups. They make us all the cash we ever see around here. That's why Micah needs help. He hunts and digs and gathers all the plants and roots we use, except for my garden stuff, which I do. Sometimes," she moved back and forth, boards creaking beneath her rockers, "sometimes I think the Lord might have sent us children. But he didn't."

"Bess!" The doctor's voice brought her to her feet instantly. "Bess, come here. I need you."

Adam sat alone before his empty plate and tried to think. He was tired now — all of his exhilaration gone. Tired of fear — tired of running. He had his vague but stubborn plan. That could wait a little while, couldn't it? Maybe a week or so? He would consider it slowly and carefully, that plan of his, and how to carry it out — but meantime he was glad that he was needed a little by somebody, somewhere.

Chapter 12

WITH FIRE IN HER EYE Mistress Jenkens withdrew her head from the large sassafras bin. Sassafras root was the most common remedy used by Dr. Jenkens, except perhaps infusion of pine tonic, and he tried to keep a good supply of both.

"Micah," shouted his wife, "do you know this sass bin is empty?"

This day she was a fit companion for the windy blasts rattling old shake singles on the roof. Adam, brushing up the floors with a twig broom, paused to listen with a smile. By now, in his second day here, he could discount her shouts, and even enjoy them if they were not directed his way. The Jenkenses seemed to take it for granted that

Adam would stay for at least this day and another night or so. He had said nothing about it himself so far. The preoccupied doctor, looking up from a letter he was writing, pushed steel-rimmed spectacles to his forehead with one hand and replied with half a mind.

"Let me see — can I pay the grocer this week? I think he'll wait a little longer, but it's time to go into Philadelphia. We surely need cash. What did you say, Bess?" He turned toward her, frowning, "Bess, you do make such a hoorah about everything. Woman, can't you quiet down when you see I'm figuring expenses?"

For once, thought Adam, Dr. Micah wasn't amused at his wife's complaints. She stood before her husband, hands on hips, eyes flashing, "Micah, stop woolgathering and hear me. That no-good boy you had here last month, the one who made off with some of the cash money we had in the desk, remember? Well, he also didn't do the work he told you he had. I took a look in the sass bin and there weren't no roots in there at all."

"Well, I be dogged, Bess. It did seem to me the last time I got some out there was mighty little, but I thought he had left the sacks in the storeroom, maybe."

"There be no sass roots in any room. Appears he didn't dig any. Now what do we do? It's nearabout time to send this month's drugs to the city."

Instead of replying to his wife the doctor looked up at Adam over his spectacles.

"How would you feel about staying here and working for us a little while, Adam?"

Adam's answer was put slowly, but he said, "Aye, sir. I think I might — for a little while." He was surprised at the relief that flooded over him. After all, where could he find a safer spot to rest his sore feet and his sore spirit for the next week or two? Perhaps he could even save the fare for a stagecoach ticket from some town on the northern edge of the barrens to New York City?

"Then, if you will stay, bring me in some oak for this fire, Adam," said Mrs. Jenkens.

"After you get in the fire sticks," added her husband, "we'll go into the woods. Won't take long to fill my bins when a strong arm handles a second shovel and knife. No patients have come in yet today, and Bess can do what's needed upstairs. Come along."

Adam followed the tall, spare man through the barnyard and out to a field cracking in frost under their boots. Job rocked along at Adam's heels, with Dr. Micah chuckling at the sight.

Sassafras grew in the forest on a rise of sandy ground near an ice-encrusted bog. It was easy enough to dig, for this soil never really froze, and both of them used their spades steadily. Then Adam watched to see how the doctor cut roots and tossed them into gunny sacks.

"You don't look as if you could work that hard, Dr. Micah," he said.

"Reckon not, boy, old dog that I am. But I'm all bone and gristle. And there's a-plenty work in me yet."

"You've lived all your life in the pines, haven't you? How did you get your schooling?"

Micah Jenkens straightened up, rested his shovel a moment, and turned his eyes into the woods with a faraway look. "I did go to school about a month or so each winter for four years. I was free, you understand, with my ma and pa out of slavery. Then I had to stop school to start as a bog iron raiser. Those days not many children went to school at all, much less a little black boy. Not many do now. Did you see any Negroes in the Bogquake school, Adam? I thought not. But my pa, he said to me, 'Micah, you go to school till you get to be a teacher. You think a black man can't teach? Well, I heard tell of one that does up in Massachusetts somewheres. You got a good mind, son. You get it to going.'"

"Then he was killed, working as a filler." Dr. Micah's eyes seemed to glaze over. He stood loosely, arms hanging by his side, speaking slowly.

"I saw him there, pushing his barrow up the incline, and I was yelling at him, 'Pa, Ma says she wants you soon as you get off. She ain't so well today.' He heard me and waved one hand, grinning at me like he often did. With one hand only on the heavy wheelbarrow he tipped it into the open stack hole. The whole barrow fell in. He reached way over for it. He went in, too. He was burned up."

Adam dropped his shovel, mouth open, scarcely able to gasp, "He — your pa — your — fell in the — furnace stack?"

With a sad voice Dr. Micah said, "Don't know why I told you that, Adam. Never told it to anybody before but Bess. It was a long time ago. I nearbout went crazy, little as I was. I figured I had killed my pa — Ma was sick, but she went to work in the Edwardses' kitchen. Nobody ever saw a bony tyke the size I was work as I did after that, to help her and my two little brothers. Well — after a while I came to understand it wasn't my fault. The Lord God moves in mysterious ways. Accidents! Who knows why? But I never went back to school. I knew how to read and write by then, anyway."

Adam stood motionless staring at the doctor, who was

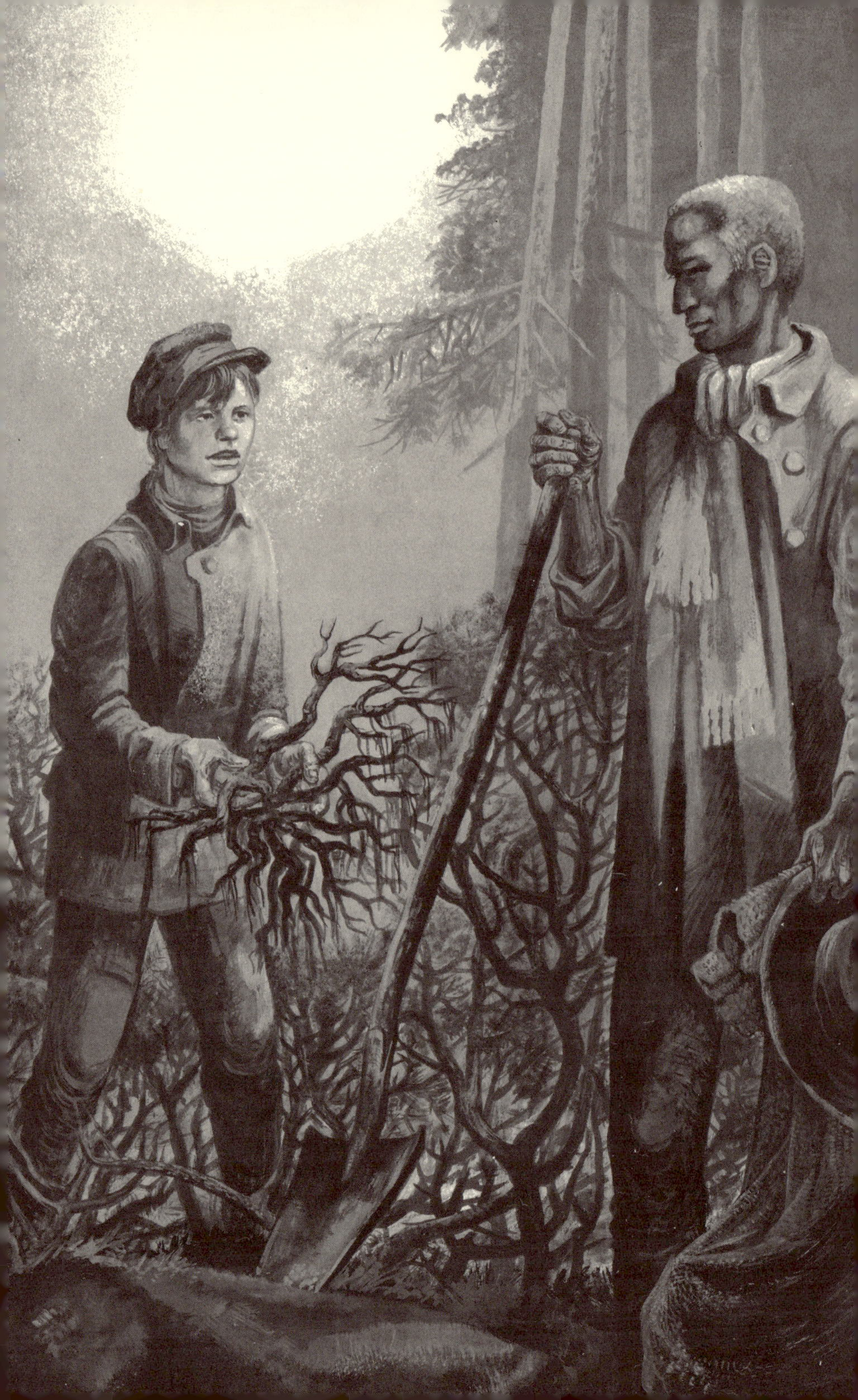

cutting sassafras roots and tossing them into the sack. Could he know about Adam's "accident"? No — that was impossible. This must be chance. Adam lifted his eyes from the bent back of the old man, and then was suddenly aware of the rustling of pine boughs, of birdsong, of the evergreen leaves of a holly bush sparkling in the sun. The piny woods were not so terrifying now. He had lived in them days and nights, alone and afraid. Now he could feel them not so much enemy as friend. The man working beside him had labored under a heavy load of guilt — and had come out from under it. That meant something special to Adam — even though Micah Jenkens had never been hunted down by the law, as he himself was. He rested on the thought that Garf would have a hard time finding his quarry here. And yet, even as he rested he heard a twig snap nearby and tensed, eyes darting that way.

As they dumped the sacks down and Adam filled the bin in the storeroom, folks were calling from the waiting room and Mistress Jenkens was whirling about doing so many things at once that she could only shout passing instructions to Adam. He tried to remember everything he was told to do and do it as well as he could, and when all of the patients had been attended to, in a quiet moment, the doctor walked into the odorous room and said, "Come here, Adam. I'll show you how to work the still. I'm making up extra distillations, pills, and powders for the pharmacy in Philadelphia." He smiled. "Boiling has to go on continuously for four days and nights. I get up all night to put more wood on the fire. Now you can tend to that chore and let an old man have his sleep."

"Micah! Need you in the office."

"Yes, Bess, I'm a-coming. I'll be right back to show you about the still."

"No need, sir. I'll figure it out."

Adam stared intently at the still. It sat on a stone hearth with a stovepipe leading smoke out through a wall. He remembered the barrels of mash and the rotten-apple smell in the Scarfy camp. This still was the same, but much smaller and older. Now what was he to do here? The ancient copper kettle had a round lid with a hole on the top. A small copper coil of pipe fit into the hole and went from there to pour pungent steam into a keg and through another pipe where, at the end, it came dripping down as a liquid. Adam reached up and pulled thoughtfully on his hair. Then he went to work putting more pine knots on the fire, setting it to roaring under the boiler. The wailing of a child in the doctor's office subsided, and suddenly Mrs. Jenkens appeared to check on the still, calling as she moved on into the kitchen beyond.

"You seem to be doing all right there. Just watch out for that old thump keg."

"Thump keg? Now what in thunder is the thump keg?" Adam murmured.

Mash was boiling vigorously, and steam was rising through the coiled copper pipe into the wooden keg, which took on a life of its own, bumping and thumping like a frenzied colt. Adam jumped for it and held it down with both hands. The coil came loose at the hole in the boiler lid. Hot mash spouted over Adam's hands and hit the ceiling.

"Oweee!" he howled, bringing both Dr. and Mrs. Jenkens into the room.

With her apron bunched around hands she moved the thump keg. Dr. Micah lifted the boiler and set it down on the hard-packed earth floor. Then he took hold of Adam's hands, saying gently, "The pain will soon pass. Bess, get me some salve from the top drawer of the cabinet — the calendula ointment — that's it — and some cloths."

Without making another sound Adam sat on a stool having his hands bound.

"Better now?"

"Aye — much better." He was ashamed of the noise he had made over the burn. "I shouldn't have let that happen. Is the still ruined?"

The doctor frowned, looking at the mess now being cleaned up by his wife. "Well — it weren't much before you got at it, Adam. I didn't mean to leave you with it the first time. That thing's our cash-maker, but I'm afeared it is nearbout done for. I built it years ago. I hope I can repair it. That load of medications has to go to the pharmacy next week."

"I'll repair it for you, Dr. Micah, or I'll get some new pipe and make you another."

"Take too long. We've got to fix this. Tomorrow you'll be able to do it." He smiled. "If I be the wonder doctor folks say I be, you'll be good as new tomorrow."

The burns were not as severe as Adam had first thought, and as pain lessened he decided he had made a great fuss over mighty little. He could fix that still on the morrow — he knew he could. Meantime he wandered about the room, trying to learn the names and appearances of dried roots, herbs, and flowers. Not for a long time had Adam been so intent on doing anything on his own — not since he had learned to read. He stared at a bookshelf — *Comley's Speller,* obviously well used, *Primitive Physic* by John Wesley, and the familiar *Journal of John Woolman* side by side with Woolman's *Considerations on the Keeping of Negroes.*

When Mrs. Jenkens came in she found him staring at a corner of the room. "Give you the shudders, don't it?" she chuckled. "Meet Old Ben, Micah's skeleton. For years he just wouldn't be satisfied till he had a skeleton to study. Well — he got him the hard and gruesome way. Ben was a pines robber who was murdered and thrown in a bog. Micah found him and brought him home. I tell you it weren't a treat having him show up here. I don't like to come near his bones at nightfall."

The front door slammed, and Dr. Micah came through the room, calling, "Adam, I'm on my way to harness up Lafayette. Want to go along?"

They rode off behind a horseman who had come for the doctor. At a farm on the edge of the pines they went into a house where the scent of sickness met them at the door. In the kitchen, on a cot beside the stove, a girl of about twelve was lying. She was so pale and thin that at first Adam thought her already dead. She opened her eyes as Dr. Micah took her wrist and asked questions of her mother. Several other women whispered in a steady buzz in the room. The big man who had come for Dr. Micah was surly.

"We had a doctor from Laurel Creek — but she only got worse. I went for you, herb doctor, only because my wife forced me. I know my little girl's a-going."

With his hand laid firmly on her forehead, Dr. Micah smiled down at the girl. Her big eyes stared into his as if she could not take them away.

"This child is not going to die," he said calmly. "Never doubt she will get well. Now, Mistress Eliza, here is what

I want you to do —" As he gave instructions he placed a bottle and a neat brown paper-wrapped powder on the table. Then he walked over to a window, pulled rags from the cracks, and opened it a few inches. Two of the women squealed and the child's mother cried.

"Don't do that! She'll die of that raw air."

"No. She won't. When this room smells clean and fresh, close it again. Not until then. Open it a little when the air gets too hot and close in here."

He moved to a pile of quilts and laid two on the girl, close up under her chin. She smiled slowly.

"You're going to get well, Beulah, aren't you?" he asked. "You and I know that."

"Yes — I'm going to get well." Her voice was stronger than Adam had expected. Dr. Micah said to her father.

"Ask these ladies to leave, and let in only her mother and you until she is able to sit up."

The man took a deep breath, then said hoarsely, "I'll do what you say. So will Eliza."

As they rode back to Crossroads Adam asked rather hesitantly, "Why do you think she will get well?"

The doctor clucked at Lafayette to get along faster. "That pine tonic of mine will have her on her feet soon. The sassafras tea and hot foot baths — and rich broth, too — all will help. The pine does most. My Indian mother taught me how to make pine needle brew — something in it sets folks on their feet — don't know what. That girl has the will to live, anyway, and given the chance, she will use it."

"Did she have swamp fever?"

"She started with that. Did you notice the marks on her skin? They were made by the Laurel Creek doctor's lancet.

133

He has taken quarts of her blood. It's a wonder she is living now. Keep him away — she will get well, now she wants to."

"I'll chop some wood," said Adam as they approached Crossroads House.

"No, not today. But you can help me get my bottles, powders, and kegs ready for a trip to the city. This one will be a light load, I'm a-feared, but I think we must get it going with what we have made. I hope to acquire the cash to buy a real still some day. Tell you what — you can drive the wagon to Philadelphia tomorrow. You know the way — you came to here."

Adam's voice was harsh and angry.

"No! I can't do that."

Micah Jenkens looked at him thoughtfully. As they pulled into the barnyard Job was throwing his ungainly self about in joyful greeting. Adam leaped out of the buggy and flung himself into the house without a word to his dog. Mrs. Jenkens called out, "Supper's ready."

But Adam went straight through and up the stairs to his room. He heard Job barking, then quiet, and a murmur of voices below, but could not catch the words. Pulling the covers over him, he lay on his bed staring at the cracked ceiling. He heard Job whining outside his door and paid no attention. After a while he slept, waking to before-dawn sounds in the kitchen, smell of woodsmoke and food frying, hearing the doctor carrying bottles, small kegs, and boxes out to the wagon. A rattle and "Gee-up, Jehosophat" as the heavy farm horse pulled out for the city.

At last Adam got up, stuffed his new, clean hose into his pocket, and went below stairs. His extra butternut cloth pants he left on a hook, along with new shirt and neckerchief. They had been given him by the Jenkenses.

"I'll be going now, Mistress Jenkens," said Adam in a low voice. She turned around.

"Oh, no, you won't, Adam Quinn. Nobody leaves here without a good, hot breakfast in his stomach. Anyway — where are you going? And why? You said only yesterday you would stay at least another week."

"I thought Dr. Micah wouldn't want me to stay on now, after I wouldn't take the load into Philadelphia for him."

"Where did you get that fool idea? He needs you. Said this morning he never had a hired boy who worked so well. We don't want to lose you, Adam." Hands on hips, face serious. "We ain't going to ask why you won't go to Philadelphia. You've got your reasons, I expect. You can stay and work here long as you want. Nobody'll fault you for not wanting to backtrack your life."

Adam took a long breath, let it out in a gust, and sat down. After breakfast Mrs. Jenkens peeled his bandages off, and he saw that the blisters were healing without much redness. She replaced salve and cloth, and he went for his ax. When he had finished chopping wood and piling it, he stared thoughtfully at the broken still, wondering if he could fix it. Job's boom followed by the farm dogs' barking signaled a caller.

"Come in here, Adam," shouted Mrs. Jenkens. He walked into the waiting room, still thinking about the broken still. She said, "This is Mr. Boyce Bollock of Tallytown. He runs the store, the jug tavern, and the jail. He's the sheriff. Says the Scarfys are taken. Mr. Bollock, this is Adam Quinn, our new hired boy."

Adam stood very still, eyes dropping, as the big man gave him a questioning look and he was hoping fervently that she would not mention his part in the Scarfy business. She sent him a sidelong glance.

"Adam's from Bogquake, Mr. Bollock. A godsend to Micah and me he is here."

The visitor ignored Adam. "I got Dr. Micah's message the other day soon as I came in, but this is the first time I could get to come out and tell him. I took George and we went right out and gathered them in. We bagged us quite a covey of renegades. Found them two Scarfys alongside their tree trunks, with Ma and the third fellow busy untying them. Got 'em all in the jail now, where they'll stay until the circuit judge comes. Much obliged to the doctor, ma'am, for catching them Scarfys. And also to whoever gave him a hand."

Did the man's eyes turn his way? Adam could not be sure. As he was leaving the sheriff paused, and this time there was no doubt that he gave Adam a long, curious look. Adam stepped uncertainly backward to the office door.

"Mistress Jenkens, that ugly three-legged brute I saw out yonder in the yard? Ain't he the critter belonged to them pines robbers?"

"Oh, could be," she said briskly. "He wandered in here and I feed him. Ugly beast, but he's friendly to us, and makes a good watchdog with that bay of his. Our other two dogs ain't fit to catch a rat, not if you give 'em the rat in front of their noses. Laziest farm dogs ever I see. They don't even fight the stray."

Mr. Bollock nodded and left with, "You feed 'em too much, ma'am. Ruins a dog."

Job bayed again, and the sheriff's horse moved away toward Tallytown. Adam's peace of mind, shattered the night before, could be held on to now only with some effort. As he worked that day he was of two minds — should he go or should he push down uneasiness and stay a little while longer? He shook his head, shoved hair out of his eyes impatiently, and said to himself, I want to stay. I'm no worse off than before. That man was satisfied.

Chapter 13

It was a bright morning, forerunner of spring, and Adam, driving the farm horse named Jehosophat, sat in an old, handmade Jersey wagon with its sheet top removed whistling "The Irish Washerwoman." By now he was used to handling both of the Jenkenses' horses, for he had been at Crossroads House nearly two weeks. On this day Mistress Jenkens had given him permission to take the wagon while Micah was away with the buggy visiting a patient at Mount Misery. She had asked no questions, although her glance was lively with curiosity. For once Adam was at peace with himself. He was sure the sheriff was satisfied about him, and his previous life seemed far away. He felt safer than he had since he had escaped from the city. He was putting off setting a day for leaving and this was easy to do since nobody mentioned the subject. Each night he told himself, "I'll decide tomorrow."

Beside him Job balanced himself with his one hind leg jutting out and his tail gently thumping the plank seat. Adam drove through Tallytown and out along the road into the pines, where he found the faint wagon tracks into the forest. Job's tail stopped wagging. They came to a bog cripple, and the wagon rolled into the edge of it and out again. Job tumbled down to the foot and crawled under the seat. They drove past thickets and emerged into the camp clearing where scent of apple mash still lingered faintly, although the moonshine still was cold and quiet. The place was strangely silent, as if a sudden catastrophe had taken its life, for the kettle of stew stood over a pile of ashes, and everything was just as he had seen it last. The dog scrambled from the wagon and leaped out to disappear in the bushes.

Adam walked slowly across the open space and found his old knapsack on the ground where it had been flung. Thrusting it over his arms he went to look at the still. Could he take this contraption apart and get it to Crossroads? He thought so. How fine a thing it would be to have a still that could double, or even triple the amount of tonics and infusions to send to the pharmacy! Adam remembered his own feeling of shame when he had seen the weary old man returning from the city, walking cheerfully into the house in his shabby clothing, with the long, red plaid scarf wound around his neck. He had said not a word about Adam's refusal to make the trip.

With the few tools he had brought Adam went to work on the still, struggling to take it apart. At first he was overwhelmed with the smell, since it contained old mash left there since the fire had gone out, but that he could get used to. For several hours he struggled with it, and at last had the coil of copper piping loosened and deposited in the wagon. Then he took the kettles and the big kegs, also. Before the sun sank behind the forest he was ready to return home, and he knew that he must get out before nightfall.

He whistled for Job, then he called. There came back to him nothing but an echo. He poked about the laurels and caught a glimpse of shaggy hide, but the dog slithered farther away, then scrambled out and ran from sight. He must be terrified by the smell of the still in the wagon, thought Adam. As sunset stained the sky he drove off, turning to whistle and call again and again. Idiotic dog! Why did he bother with him? Well — there was nothing to do about this but to return tomorrow and try to find Job.

As he made the turn with protesting wheels, shadows were closing in on the pine barrens on either side of the road. A huge, dark thing sprang from some bushes into the wagon, sending Adam bouncing into the air with a terrified yell. As he came down on the seat and tried to quiet the alarmed horse, he shouted furiously, "Job! Did you have to scare the liver and lights out of me?"

The Jenkenses came outside hurriedly at sound of wagon wheels, exclaiming loudly, "What're you trying to do to us, Adam? Scare us into our graves?"

"We were fretting about you, boy, not knowing where you were."

"I'm sorry, sir." For a quick moment Adam wondered if

they thought he had stolen the rig and absconded with it. "I've got a surprise for you. Look in there!"

They came to peer into the wagon as Job got out of it as fast as he could jump.

"Lord, what is it? It stinks enough to send a body reeling."

"The still?" said the herb doctor. "You brought the Scarfys' still here?"

"Why not use it? I can get it going, I know I can, and we can make more drugs than you ever did before."

Dr. Micah chewed his lower lip, frowning, then his face creased in a smile. "Well, I reckon it's all right. Scarfys won't have use for it again. What a mess of pine tonic that will make! Yes, sir — it will! Think you can get it to work, Adam?"

"I can try."

Early next day Adam set to work cleaning out a shed. He installed a stovepipe in the wall and on the hard earth floor laid a fireproof base of flat stones. Then he boiled applejack odor and taste out of the vessels, cleaned them over and over with sand and lye and rinsed them in the stream. April days stayed warm and the water ran free. Even this overlong winter was gone.

Suddenly the thought struck him that he ought to be on his way in this warmer weather. And yet — if the new still worked well, how could Dr. Micah gather enough pine needles and roots to make full use of it? Where would he get the time, let alone the strength? No, Adam could not leave just now. He must stay long enough to get in large supplies from the forest and to help his friends store up the essence of earth-grown life in bottles and kegs. Adam thought of the furious aim in his own life, and for a long moment he didn't care about anything else. Why had he ever taken hold of the belief that he must stay here and tie himself to such work?

Scowling, he went for pine needles, hatchet and sack in hand, dog at heel. All day, as he chopped and stripped boughs, Adam was vastly troubled. He was torn first one way and then another. When he came in, steps slow and disconsolate, the doctor said, "You have a liking for the piny wood now, I think. It grows on a body. There be prettier places, and easier ones — none that sinks in so good to ease a troubled spirit."

"Aye."

"Before you know it you'll get to be a piney," laughed Mistress Jenkens.

For a long moment Adam stood silently, pulling on his hair as he thought, and then he said abruptly, "Would you want me to stay the summer?"

"We would," said Dr. Micah with a sudden smile. And, "Glory be!" shouted his wife.

Adam spent the next few days putting the still together. The first time he fired it steam hissed out of cracks in the joint where the coil of pipe was fitted to the hole in the boiler top, and Adam, recalling the thump keg, hastily got the boiler off the fire. When it had cooled he found some new rivets and fastened them securely. As steam passed through the coil and pine concentrate dripped steadily into the keg, Adam looked at the happy faces of the Jenkenses and felt the same excitement that had stirred him when he found that he could read.

One night as he rested beside the kitchen fire, legs stretched out to the warmth and Job nearby close to the ashes, he heard a deep voice calling and the front door opening. The Jenkenses looked quickly at each other and without a word hurried out. Adam heard them talking but could not distinguish words, then she came in to hastily wrap cornbread, cooked ham, and a piece of cheese in a clean cloth and tie it with a jerk. Silently she handed it to her husband as he came through on his way to the barn. Adam sat up straighter.

"Can I harness your horse, Dr. Micah? Want me to go with you?"

"No, Adam. Not this time. I'll do it myself."

He was gone with a quick step, the bundle of food in his hand. Adam said uneasily to Mrs. Jenkens, "Is something wrong?"

"Don't you bother yourself, Adam." She picked up some sewing, but tonight her fingers were clumsy; she pricked herself, then sewed rapidly. Her eyes found Adam's. "Just don't talk about this night. Not to nobody at all. It has nothing to do with you." At last, when Adam put another log on the fire, her voice was low and gloomy.

"Wind's coming up. I can feel it through the chinks. Bad night for Micah to go. Hear the pines moaning? Pretty soon we'll pick up screams and agonies out in the spongs."

"That's just the crying of cedar boughs scraping so close together."

"That's what you say, but who knows, sometimes maybe it's more than that, too? I've heard the Jersey Devil myself, more'n once. Never seen him, though. Don't want to, I can tell you. But I know folks that have seen him."

"Dr. Micah says there is no such a thing as the Jersey Devil."

"Micah's fearless. He hasn't a nerve in his skinny body.

But I know there is a devil in the pines — maybe more'n one. Folks in Tallytown tell me they have seen the Jersey Devil himself on a wild night, with the wind whishing in from the ocean, blowing sand from the dunes all the way up here. And heard him, too. Screeching like a congregation of owls. Why, on such a night ships toss and crash on the shore, lured by lights lit by the Jersey Devil. Adam, you believe in signs?"

"Sometimes," he said cautiously. "Everybody does. But those lights luring ships to destruction are more likely lit by wreckers on the dunes looking to advantage themselves by salvage."

"Everybody believes in signs but my man Micah. He says the Lord protects those who go their way without living by signs and portents. But I do. Now — take some signs — like seeing the first serpent after the new year starts. You kill it and you defeat your enemies till the next new year."

"When I was working in the bogs I saw many a snake, but I didn't kill a one. I got away fast as greased pigs. I'm a city chap — and I don't get over being scared of snakes."

"Then, Adam," she sighed gustily, "you've got your enemies to contend with for the rest of the year. No fooling about that, though don't tell Micah I said so, as he wouldn't bear with me talking that way. He's read so much, you know. Never went to school a lot, but he's the most educated man in all the piny woods. He's borrowed books from about every house has one in down-Jersey. He taught me to read, which is more than most men or women can do, but that's far as I got. You like to read, I can see that. Maybe it'll benefit you one day. Go on to bed, Adam. Micah will be back soon."

Lying in bed listening to the wind in bog cedars, Adam heard the buggy come in and then the slow step mounting the stairs.

Next day was as usual. Adam asked no questions. How could he when they asked none of him? He thought they must surely suspect that he was on the run from the law, yet he did not know that they did. Nevertheless, Adam could not help but wonder what errand took the herb doctor out at night, and so secretly, and it was only after some weeks that he was told that the man who came like a shadow was Micah's brother, Henry, who ran an Underground Railroad station for runaway slaves from the South. Micah went when they needed medical attention for sickness or injuries.

At breakfast one morning, after such a journey the night before, the weary doctor, glancing at Adam, began to talk of it, telling him that he supposed Adam must know that, although New Jersey had abolished slavery by law eleven years before this time, there was still a great deal of sympathy with slavery in more prosperous parts of this state than the barrens. Lawless slave runners operated even in the pines now and then, as folks said the Scarfys had done at times.

"I've known free black people to be taken and sold to slave markets, and their families never heard of them again. Not often around here, as most pineys don't like slavers and will stop them if given a chance, even when pineys break the law by not turning runaway slaves in to be returned to the South. You've heard of the Fugitive Slave Act, haven't you? It's a federal law that says slaves must be returned to their masters. Pineys treat Negroes like themselves in the barrens. After all, they or their forebears were often as not renegades, or they escaped from something or other themselves.

"That's why I don't want you mixed into underground railroad activities, Adam. You've got troubles of your own, if I'm not mistaken, of some kind or other — so I can't have you taking a chance of getting jailed for helping slaves get away to the northern border. And now, Adam, we'll get horehound to make drops, and then dig pleurisy root. After that you and Mrs. Jenkens can boil up some more peppermint syrup, and make some boneset tea infusion. Takes a lot to satisfy that new still. Check on the ipecac, Adam, and on snakeroot stock — and we can do with more skunk cabbage, too. It's just come up big enough. And don't forget to fill the pine needle sacks. That ought to keep you busy."

"Next time I go to the city I want to get more saffron and ipecac in trade for pine tonic — and swamp fever requires quinine bark. We don't grow it here."

"Keep that boy busy for a month of Sundays," laughed Mrs. Jenkens, "and, Adam — in your spare time how about chopping me some kindling?"

Chapter 14

THE WAGON rattled merrily on Fork-ed Road, jolting through sleepy Tallytown just after daylight on an early summer day, its creaks and groans making background accompaniment to a tune whistled cheerfully. The day was cool, sunny, and glistening on tree, bush, and blossom — the sun even so brave as to poke sharp golden fingers deep into dark cedar bogs. Job laid his unlovely jaw upon his paws, resigned to the whistle that hurt his ears. Adam stopped his tune to consider his instructions. The doctor had said, "Now, Adam, I want you to get me a whole mess of plants. Start with a goodly supply of wild carrots, catnip for baby tea, and some pleurisy roots for 'stitches and burning.' I need more camomile leaves for my 'getting well patients,' and some, but not a lot, of red skunk cabbage to boil up with spikenard for cough balsam."

"You won't find pleurisy roots close by," he continued, "so you had better take the wagon and go yonder to here for all of it."

"You mean yonder to where?" Adam was puzzled once again over piney talk. He knew that to a piney *here* did not mean where he was at the moment. The word *there* seemed not to figure in barrens language.

The doctor said easily and patiently, in spite of his busy day, "Go through town down Fork-ed Road. Then turn at the off point on the on side — you'll find a nice lot — and bring in some wild indigo also, if so be you find any."

Leaving Tallytown Adam smiled as he remembered that in piney talk a "point" was the fork of a road, and the place where several small roads came together was known as a "fingerboard." Mrs. Jenkens never said she wanted a rest, but always, as with all pineys, she spoke of it as wanting "a little leisure." In Bogquake Adam had learned to make use of terms strange to him, but in the deep barrens there were many more. It took some thought to figure out at first that when a patient at Crossroads House said, "I've got a misery in my stomach anyhow," she meant, "I'm sick in my stomach nowadays."

As for the word *nice* — Why, thought Adam, it is used so often and for so many different things that it is the best catchall word I've ever heard. Unless something was downright bad — it was "nice." He found himself saying, "I did a nice work today — that well gives nice water — he's nice and sick — my dog is nice and ugly."

Adam had come to feel a deep affection for the doctor, and great respect. Micah Jenkens did "nice" medical work in the pines for everybody. When he had no time to spare, he had taken time to teach Adam the names, the looks, and the qualities of countless plants — their roots, leaves, flowers — and especially their uses for healing. Foxglove strengthened the heart. Sassafras purified the blood. Wild indigo was a stimulant. The doctor gave medicines made only from natural growing plants, trees, and certain fungus and did not believe in chemical compounds or other man-made drugs.

Dr. Micah Jenkens treated his patients with his own remedies — with his own spirit — and, perhaps most important of all, he always knew at once what was causing the illness. Adam realized that not many physicians had Dr. Micah's ability to diagnose a patient's trouble so accurately.

The wagon turned into a road to the left that was more a track, and bumped over the ground until Adam pulled in Jehosophat and jumped out to fill the sacks. He circled his eyes about and observed most of the plants that he needed. There was also a grove of butternut trees not far away. The herb doctor seldom raised blisters to cure a lung disease, but once in a while he did think it necessary to bring up a blister on a bad chest. For this he used either mustard plaster or butternut bark.

Butternut trees did not grow close by Crossroads, so Adam decided to bring back some bark. He peeled pieces carefully, taking care to follow instructions to get the inner layer, also, and to take it from the north side of the tree down near the root. He would not take much, for he knew that to make it effective after soaking in vinegar the inner layer must be at least fairly fresh.

Sacks filled with various plants, Adam was getting hungry, and when he had dumped them into the wagon he decided to leave. Just then he noticed that the sluggish stream beyond a thicket to his right was covered with sphagum moss along its edges. Dr. Jenkens never had too much moss, for the stuff held water like a sponge, even after it was squeezed over and over, and the doctor said that it had an acid, antiseptic quality to heal sores and wounds.

Adam was pulling off his boots and rolling up his pants legs when he thought he heard a noise. He listened as Job rose to growl. What kind of animal would make that low, agonized sound? Job growled again and moved toward the thicket. Adam followed to grab Job by his shaggy neck.

Hidden in the bushes he saw a human form as motionless as death. Adam shoved the dog back and knelt, feeling for a pulse in the wrist. It was there, though feeble. He straightened up and stared at the black man clad in ragged clothing which scarcely covered his emaciated body. A low groan escaped the pale lips. Adam jumped up and went for water, bringing it back in a gourd from the wagon. The man opened his eyes, and seeing a stranger, recoiled, terrified.

"It's all right. I won't hurt you. Can you sit up?"

With Adam's help the man slowly raised himself and turned his head from side to side as if to clear it. Adam bit his lip, thinking hard, as the man began to shake so violently that his teeth chattered.

"You've got breakbone fever, I think, with that chill. I'll take you to Crossroads House."

And yet when he tried to help him up and get him to the wagon the sick man jerked away and staggered to his feet, only to fall again into the bushes. Adam hoisted the limp arms about his own neck and raised the man to his back. As he got him into the wagon, with his head on a sack of skunk cabbage leaves, Adam said, "Now don't fear. Dr. Micah Jenkens will help you. I'm taking you to him."

The man's eyes stopped rolling in terror as he heard the name of the herb doctor, and he spoke in a whisper, "Want — help —"

Adam considered. There was little chance that anyone here in the barrens would turn in an escaped slave — that is, no one but those pines robbers who were sometimes willing to collect money for carrying them to Delaware Bay to be returned to the South. Still and all, he had better be careful. You couldn't tell when you might run into a renegade.

The sun was low as Adam, working fast and furiously, cut enough pine boughs to cover the sick man completely. Job kept growling suspiciously, but jumped to the seat and settled down as they drove as fast as possible into Fork-ed Road toward Tallytown and on to Crossroads House.

Adam slowed Jehosophat as he came into Tallytown and glanced around to see the sheriff standing in front of his office.

"Evening, Mr. Bollock."

"Hey, you chap — what are you doing here this time of evening?"

"Sir, I'm, — I'm only coming back with a load of stuff for Dr. Jenkens."

A low groan and the sound of chattering teeth rose to Adam's ears and he raised his voice and turned to Job, shouting, "You stop that noise, dog! Stop it, I say!"

The big man moved over toward the wagon, glancing into it, and Adam held his breath for fear that another groan would come from beneath the pine boughs.

"All right, you chap. Seems to me something's funny — somehow —" He reached up to scratch his head. "I got a feeling about you — you ain't nohow what you 'pear to be, I'll take my oath on that fact. All right, then, get them boughs to the doctor."

Adam heaved a monstrous sigh as he drove on, and he did not feel safe until he turned into the farmyard and drew up at the door.

They carried the man, now babbling in delirium, upstairs, where Mrs. Jenkens bathed him with cool water, and on her husband's orders began to drop sudorific liquid into his mouth with a teaspoon. This remedy for malaria, and many other diseases, was made of a teacup each of vinegar, whiskey, and sweet water, and Micah Jenkens relied on it to cool a fever. The doctor himself administered medicine made of quinine bark soaked in warm water and put the patient's feet to soak in a basin of ashes and warm water.

The next morning Adam worked with the fresh plants, stripping, soaking, boiling, and dumping pine needles into the still. As he put new supplies in their places he was careful to read the labels each time, for the first instruction the doctor had given him was never to get the wrong herbs into a drawer or bin. There were a few plants that were deadly poison — and they were prepared and given only by the doctor himself. Adam must always recognize them when growing, as well as in the bins. These included mandrake root, swamp hellebore, and pokeroot. When used in minute quantities, and for certain illnesses, they could cure. Adam knew exactly how they looked and gave them due respect.

The black man, so emaciated that he was all bones with skin stretched so tightly over them, hard chills subsiding, gradually came out of his fever and was able to take soft food from Mrs. Jenkens. Adam visited him as often as he was allowed, talked to him of his own adventures fleeing through the pine barrens, and even got a small smile out of him after a description of how he had run from the quick-on-the-trigger charcoal men. Yet the sick man said very little himself. Dr. Micah told Adam that William was not much older than Adam was, that he had run away from a plantation in South Carolina, and had escaped capture many times. He had been without food for days. It seemed something of a miracle that he had found his way into the barrens at all here in the North. And then the doctor said, "That would have been the end of William, there in that spong, if you hadn't found him and brought him to us. We thank you, and he thanks you."

Adam flushed and yanked on his hair as he said, "I don't want thanks, Dr. Micah, not from anybody. I happened on him. I'm glad I did, sir. Tell him not to thank me."

The doctor's eyes crinkled with a smile at Adam's embarrassment. "All right then — I'll tell William if he tries to give you thanks you'll run like a deer."

They held a celebration with a special dinner the day that William was able to walk downstairs and eat with them, and Adam was pleased to see that, although he still said little, William was calm, unafraid, and confident with the herb doctor near.

One morning, when Adam had slept like a stone all

night, hearing nothing, he came down to find both Dr. Micah and William gone.

"Mistress Jenkens," said Adam miserably, "I brought William here, and I thought I could help get him away to the Underground Railroad station. Dr. Micah doesn't trust me, does he?" Once again he felt like an outcast.

Bess Jenkens came over and put a hand on his, saying in her warm voice, "Now, you know we trust you, Adam. But Micah won't get you mixed up in this — when you've got troubles of your own."

She turned to the stove, "Sit down, boy. I've got some hot cornbread with butter dripping down the sides, and a jug of honey a-spoiling to be eaten."

Chapter 15

Adam primed the pump and drank long from water gushing into a gourd. He wiped his mouth with the back of his hand and looked at the dark rim of forest encircling Crossroads House and its few fields.

"That's the best tasting water ever I drank," he said to the herb doctor, who was passing on his way to the house.

"You're used to city water, and this water be the purest on earth, I do believe. Under this whole pine forest I am sure there is a deep lake of cold water. You appear to be learning to appreciate the piny woods." He paused to get himself a drink.

Adam, ax in hand, looked at the forest again. "Aye. It's hard to remember how scared to death I was of the barrens when I ran away from Bogquake."

He slapped a mosquito on his neck, wiped his hand on his pants leg, and attacked the woodpile. His thoughts ran to Bogquake, and he wondered if Tranquility was still there. Or had she journeyed to Indian country beyond the western mountains? Last month when Dr. Micah had gone to Bogquake Adam had asked him to tell Mr. Walter Hobson that he, Adam, was working for the herb doctor. On his return Dr. Micah said only that he had delivered the message and that no word had been sent back.

And what of Kip? He must be well into his down-Jersey rounds by this time. "Wish he would travel this way, but he won't. Nobody in the deep barrens has money to buy pictures." Still, Kip had said once that sometimes he took a shortcut through the pines — and yet Adam knew he would never pass by here on Fork-ed Road.

He went into the woods, herb sack in hand, dog at heel as always. Wild cherry bark was easy to find, he thought, as he stripped it down, but he had to prowl about and look for wild indigo and pipsissewa leaves. He pulled a candy plant, brushed off the root, and chewed it slowly, savoring the taste of sweet peppermint on the tongue, and he favored his eyes with sight of a carpet of golden bell blossoms spread across a wild meadow. The pine barrens seemed bursting with early summer. At his feet Adam saw tiny clumps of violets — and there was a lady's-slipper, or a whippoorwill shoe, as Bess Jenkens called it. He looked up at the sound of a joyous honking, thinking that it was still spring after all, in spite of the warmth, for there were arrows of geese in the sky pointing to the north. A movement on his left set Job to barking, and Adam caught a glimpse of a gray fox scooting up the bent trunk of a tree.

The stark gray-green world of winter in which he had

wandered, fearful and hopeless, now rejoiced in white starry azaleas and swamp pinks and in so many kinds of tiny wild orchids that he could not remember their names, although the doctor had named some of them off for him. He turned his steps homeward, once putting down his sack to stoop, part the bushes in a damp spot, and look at small curly ferns thrusting tendrils toward the sun.

Even a cedar bog, its dark water slowly and ceaselessly quaking under sphagnum moss, seemed good to him now. He must come for sphagnum moss soon, for Dr. Micah used a lot of it for bandaging wounds — he often said it had healing properties in itself and was a better bandage than man could make. He watched beavers popping out of their rounded houses, noses and alert eyes fixed on him, slapping the water with their tails in a sound like musket shots as they dove out of sight. He stayed well back from them, for Dr. Micah had said, "Adam, I do think the pine barrens breed the fiercest beavers in the world. It is said that nothing in the woods will tackle a beaver, except maybe a wild boar, and he'll get himself chewed up if he tries."

Adam went back to Crossroads House as if he belonged there and to the forest surrounding it. That evening he sat with the Jenkenses on their front porch slapping mosquitoes, taking it for granted that man was meant to be eaten by insects. Dr. Micah talked a little about a lumberjack he had visited that day, a man who had been pinned by a falling tree, a fellow who lived alone in a shack on Sundew Creek. The doctor was telling them that old Jacob, who must be ninety if he was a day, had a broken bone in his leg, but he was in good spirits and, Micah was sure, would heal slowly but without trouble.

"Bess," he said, "maybe you ought to fix him up some cooked vittles and Adam take it out to — who's that coming in from Fork-ed Road?"

"That's Mr. Bollock. Now I wonder what he wants with us?"

The barking of the dogs, in which Job's bay nearly drowned out the others, stopped at a shout from Adam. The sheriff came to the porch with deliberate step. Abruptly, on impulse, Adam got up and went indoors. He hesitated, wishing he had not done so, for the man had probably seen him. He stood still a moment, then moved into the front room where he could hear.

"Will you sit, Mr. Bollock?" asked Micah. "Rest yourself a spell."

"Fine evening, ma'am," said the sheriff. "Bit warm, though. Don't mind if I sit a bit."

Creaks and groans from the chairs as the big man dropped into one and the others resumed their rocking.

"Well, Dr. Micah, I keep thinking about that ugly dog you got hanging around here. Can't get it off my mind." Pause, long drawn out. "Tell you the truth — I don't feel easy about you folks. That stray fellow you hired — he's still here? Thought I saw him just now."

"Adam? Yes, of course. He's working for me this summer."

"Well — I just wonder what you know about him?"

"We know enough. He's a good worker."

"Doctor — you and Mistress Bess here — you be the best liked folks in the piny woods, I reckon. But you ain't got your feet planted on the ground secure-like. You be real trusting folks. I got a feeling you don't know anything about that big young chap. He just showed up here, I'll wager, and you took him in like you do every kit and kaboodle of a man, woman, or child comes around needing, or saying they do."

"Adam's all right, Mr. Bullock. You can take my word for that."

"Your word's good. Still and all, I'm not easy in my mind about that young chap. I'm making inquiries about him. I'll just tell you I suspect him to be a smuggler. Else why does that dog hang about with him? Part of the Scarfy gang that chap be, I'll wager on it. Got no proof yet — but I'm working on it. For all you know, doctor, you and your missus could be bloody murdered in your bed one night. Forewarned is forearmed, as they say. Be careful."

He got up and Adam heard him walking down the steps. At the bottom he called, "You watch out now! Take care!"

Adam no longer wanted to go back to the porch. Instead he went quietly up to bed. When he dropped off to sleep his dreams were bad. He woke himself up more than once crying out — and the last time he lay quivering with a word that he was sure he had shouted, "Murderer!"

He listened and heard nothing from the bedroom where the Jenkens slept. Should he leave now? He realized that he did not want to go. After a time he reminded himself that the sheriff could find no evidence that he was a smuggler, for he wasn't. How could he discover that Adam was a fugitive from the law in Philadelphia? It was more than a year since he had fled the city. The chase must have let up by now. Adam decided to keep his word and stay until autumn. And as for danger — it was present for him anywhere he went, even if his crime was old and the trail growing cold.

It was the first of the month, and for three days it rained.

On the fourth morning Adam arose in darkness, before he heard the Jenkenses stirring, and crept down the stairs. He lit a lantern and made his way to the shed where the still was housed and carried kegs outside. Then, taking the lantern to the bottle room he put out containers of medicines. As dawn appeared Adam had Jehosophat hitched to the wagon and was loading it for the city. Dr. Micah came out, saying, "I see you have me fixed up for my journey, Adam. Mr. Walker is depending on me, and he expects me now that the weather has improved. It does worry me to get in later than the first Monday of every second month — and here it is Friday. Come along in, Adam, and we'll get breakfast inside us. I'll pay you your week's wages now."

The sun was scarcely poking its face above the pines when the doctor drove out of the farmyard. Adam was standing by the gate holding it open for the wagon, with Job beside him. Job swayed from side to side barking loudly. A young boy, riding barebacked, galloped up and drew to a halt before the wagon. Mrs. Jenkens was already running toward them.

Gathering his breath the boy said, "Dr. Micah, come quick. Pa stopped in to see old Jacob. Over on Sundew Creek — says he's bad. Pa thinks he's got gangrene in his leg. Old Jacob is raving in his head with fever, too."

The doctor slowly got down from the wagon. His wife reached them and Micah told her of the emergency. The boy turned his horse. Adam thought he had never seen the doctor so disturbed. Mrs. Jenkens spoke loudly, "Adam, go hitch up Lafayette to the buggy. Micah's got to go to Jacob. Micah — I'll drive the load in to Philadelphia. Now don't you say no to me. I can drive the wagon well's you can."

Micah started to call to the boy — but he was already riding back the way he had come in a cloud of dust, taking it for granted that Dr. Micah would go at once. The herb doctor protested, "Bess, I don't want you to do that. You can drive the wagon all right, I never said you couldn't. But you don't know the way to Philadelphia. You've never been there in your life. How would you find Walker's Pharmacy?"

"Now you looka here, Micah Jenkens, I can —" She broke off and they both turned toward the road. The wagon was moving away toward Tallytown, seat rattling in tune with the shaking and jiggling of kegs and bottles. Adam was urging the farm horse on, flapping the reins up and down, shouting, "Gee up there, Jehosophat!"

The shaggy dog began to bark, and Adam did not turn his head to look back at the astonished pair standing in the road.

When he had left Tallytown behind he came to the fork leading to the shortest route to the Delaware River. He stopped and sat awhile looking at the main road, thinking that if he continued on it sooner or later he would come to Bogquake. Why not? It would take only a few hours longer than the other way.

"Gee up, Jehosophat!"

All the way, as the road through the barrens stretched out before him, Adam's thoughts were on the schoolhouse in the iron town. Had Tranquility gone into the western wilderness? As he drove into Bogquake the roar and blast of furnace and mills smote his ears and made him wince.

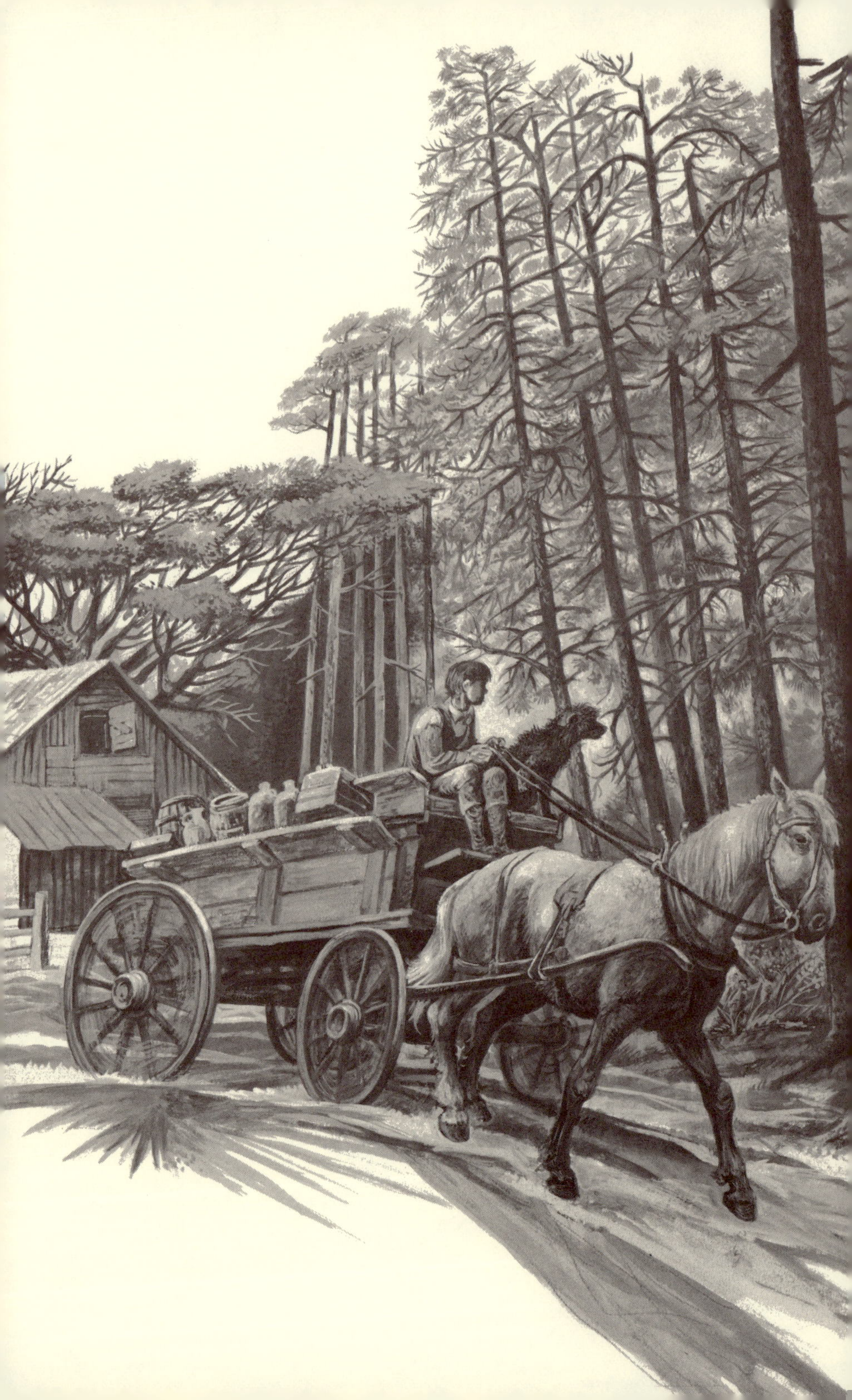

In the quiet of the pines he had forgotten how the town shook with continuous noise.

He drew up before Friends Meeting House and saw the door burst open to let a wave of children through, with their teacher reprimanding them loudly for their behavior. Adam waited until she had brought her charges to a proper calm and dismissed them. Then she turned and saw him.

"Adam Quinn! Is it really thee?"

She stepped out in her bonnet and shawl, holding out both hands. Adam flushed as he grasped them and then dropped them again. Job lifted his head to bay. Tranquility gave a small shriek, "What — what kind of beast is that?"

"Down, Job! Go to the wagon." Adam sternly ordered the dog back in and returned, grinning a little.

"That's my dog, Quillie. He looks like some kind of a bad dream, but he's harmless."

They sat on a bench, door open to the warm air outside and Adam said, "Tranquility — last month — did you get a message I sent to Mr. Hobson by the kindness of Dr. Micah Jenkens?"

"Was I meant to have a message? I didn't know that."

"Aye — aye — I thought it best to send word of where I was to Mr. Hobson, who employed me. And Dr. Micah was coming here. I — well — I —" he finished lamely, "I thought they would tell you, the Hobsons, I mean."

"Why did thee think so? And what made thee believe such a message would mean anything to me?" Her voice was cool and aloof, as if she was sorry to have been carried away so at sudden sight of him, and yet — was that a sideways glance she was giving him? Adam squirmed, his face growing red, and he yanked hard on his hair.

"I thought you would want to know. If I had thought otherwise I would not have asked."

She burst out laughing. "Adam, thee is a goose, indeed. I was glad to know thee to be alive and well. We had been sorely concerned ever since that night thee made a clandestine retreat. Why did thee go like a thief in the night?"

"I can't tell you that. Not now. Someday perhaps I can. If I am still hereabouts to tell anything. I don't know what may happen to me yet, although I am easier in spirit in the barrens."

"I welcome the news that thee is easier in spirit, Adam. I must tell thee that I may go away soon. Although I am very young for the work, I have had my wish granted to join a mission approved by Philadelphia Meeting. The word to go may come any day."

Adam drew in a deep breath, then let it out suddenly. All along he had known she meant to do this, and yet he had hoped she would change her mind.

"Then I'll say farewell, and Godspeed to you. I hope your journey will be good and you will bring many a red man's soul to the Quakers." He was afraid she would be angry at the bitterness in his voice, but she said gently, "Adam, will thee spend the night at the farm? My mother and father will give thee welcome."

"Thankee, I cannot. I am on my way to sell remedies for Dr. Jenkens and must be off to the city. Give my respects to your mother and father, and to the Hobsons. Goodbye, Tranquility. If I do not see you again I wish you success in saving heathens."

She drew back, hurt now at his sharp tone, and then said in a low troubled voice, "Farewell, Adam Quinn. And God go with thee."

After stopping at the store to buy bread and cheese, he turned onto a different road from that passing by the Willowby farmstead, although it took an hour more to reach Long-a-Coming this way. The town he passed through without stopping. Was that a hint of tears in her eyes? He was furious with himself for hurting her. Job leaned toward him and moved a huge, wet tongue over his hand.

"Well, dog," said Adam, "I think you and I are of one and the same sort. We are outcasts. We have been much put upon, lost, and alone. Yet we go on struggling. If backed into a corner in the 'City of Brotherly Love' we will defend ourselves — but not unless we have to." The words tasted sour in his mouth.

Chapter 16

A<small>FTER A NIGHT'S SLEEP</small> in the wagon Adam and Job ate bread and cheese left from the night before, drank from a cold stream, and embarked on the final leg of their journey. With the rising sun they joined increasing numbers of carts and wagons heading for the city market. Adam glanced quickly at every rig, first at the driver to see if anybody appeared to recognize him, then, out of curiosity, at the loads they carried. Some Jersey carters hauled iron objects, and others glass blown into jugs, goblets, and pieces such as he had seen in the market in the past. He remembered glass walking canes, and once he had seen a high-crowned hat made of glass. Men and women taking in vegetables, fruits, chickens, and pigs never even glanced his way.

When he reached Camden and Cooper's Ferry Adam moved slowly along the line of barges waiting for passengers. He saw no sign of the man he had escaped on his trip to Jersey when he had manned the sweep. Nevertheless, he moved far down the line and took his wagon on board the last flatboat moored there. Glad enough he was, too, that he had been paid his wages the day before, and had still jingling in his shirt all that was left after buying food. He took it out to count it and saw to his relief that, although paying a bargeman would leave him nothing, these few coins were enough to get him over the river.

When the boat pulled away from shore Adam could not help a laugh as he thought of his flight from the irate flatboatman.

Holding his horse's head, he turned to look at the city growing larger and larger. Swarming Water and Front Streets were as crowded as he remembered them. He could pick out easily the big brick building housing the Jervis Shipping Company, and his thoughts were somber. He remembered Old Adam, the high voice, and the pounding of that silver cane. With burning eyes he hardened his resolve once more. In the autumn he would go north to educate himself to take revenge on that evil old man.

He knew the way to Walker's Pharmacy on Chestnut Street, for he had walked past it many times, and yet the route was difficult for he was uneasy, darting his eyes first to one side and then to the other, afraid that he would hear a constable shouting, "I've caught you, Adam Quinn!"

When he drew up before the narrow shop with three tall bottles of colored water in the window, under the sign bearing a mortar and pestle, Adam felt only relief that he had gained it safely.

Mr. Walker was pleased with the large load of drugs, and he said, "Tell Dr. Micah I will take all of the infusion of pine needle I can get. No one else makes it, and it has a good sale to physicians here. That is true as well of his sassafras tea, the best available. And people also buy both of these without the advice of doctors. Yes — I believe he wants Peruvian quinine bark in trade for some of these, and also some Spanish saffron. Say to him that this bark is the better kind for treating swamp fever than the last shipment I had."

"Here is the money for the doctor. Would you like to take it in a deerskin sack? You can have one of these — since you seem not to be supplied with a money pouch, young man."

Adam drove through the streets where familiar shop signs swung above passing vehicles, remembering to duck under a big one so as not to crack his skull. Now he was easier, for with load delivered and money in his pouch, he could get away fast if necessary.

He even left himself enjoy the sight of people crowding together, talking as they pushed and shoved their way among stalls and tables in front of shops. His eyes found a bookstore and he pulled up Jehosophat before it, told Job to stay, and jumped down to look at the old volumes tumbled in bins on the sidewalk. When last he had seen this shop he had stood mutely before it, staring hungrily at unintelligible lines of type marching along like a row of unknown soldiers. He picked up a book and read the title aloud with delight shining in his face, *The Medical Botany Book, a Pharmaco — poe-ia —* that one wasn't easy — *of Healing Plants, Roots, Blossoms, Their Uses and the Diseases Cured by Their Application Internally and Exter-*

nally. To read that title was an accomplishment, and he had done it!

"Young man," said a sober sounding voice next to him. "Does thee care deeply for learning?"

Adam turned to look at an elderly Quaker gentleman, "Aye, sir."

"Then never let any man nor circumstance stop thee. Learning is a lifetime thing."

The man moved away with a smile and disappeared in the throng. As Adam turned to the dusty book again, money jingled in the deerskin pouch under his shirt. He drew it out slowly and, book in hand, went inside the dim little shop.

"I'll take this book," he said, as if he bought books each day without giving the purchase a thought. Then, holding it as if it were a basket of fresh eggs, Adam shoved the pouch back inside his shirt and climbed into the wagon.

As he did so he glanced at a shining black carriage with open top drawn alongside him in the crush of vehicles. His breath caught sharply in his throat. Seated in the carriage was a shriveled figure in old-fashioned black clothing too large for the wizened body. The head wobbled, and clawlike hands resting on knees quivered as if they were the last withered leaves on a dying oak. A silver-headed cane rested beside him. The face was half hidden beneath a broad-brimmed hat, and yet Adam knew it. He felt the book beside him on the seat. He wanted to pick it up and shout with all of his might, "See, Old Adam! I can read this book. You couldn't stop me."

He could easily leap into that carriage from his wagon. He could grasp that evil old man and shake him until his bones rattled and fell apart. For a long few minutes the carriage stood beside Adam, waiting for the way ahead to open.

He dropped the reins and stood up, eyes burning. As if he had felt the heat of those eyes the old man raised his head and his hat fell off. The shrunken face lifted, and dim eyes stared up as if with a blind man's look. A thin thread of saliva trickled from a corner of the grimacing lips. The head jerked as if it were a dead pod on a stalk flicked by the careless hand of a boy.

Adam stood speechless. Then he slowly sat down and picked up his reins. He was shaken with the realization that Old Adam had escaped him. He had thought Adam Jervis to be Lucifer himself, a mighty devil who would live forever doing his evil will. Now he knew that nothing he could do, or say, would reach his grandfather. He must leave him to God to deal with — or to the devil.

The packed-in vehicles ahead began to move, the coachman urged on his pair of sleek horses, and still Adam sat there unmoving, reins slack in hand. A carter, unable to get going behind him, swore loudly and was echoed angrily by others. Job began to bay. Adam let out a lungful of air and called, "Gee up, Jehosophat. We're going home!"

That night he slept like a log in the wagon, untroubled by dreams, with Job resting heavily on his feet. He awoke to pine scent and sunshine, and he drove on whistling "The Irish Washerwoman." The sun was setting as they pulled into the barnyard at Crossroads House, and an aroma of frying eggs and baking soda bread welcomed them.

Chapter 17

Micah Jenkens cut short Adam's explanation for borrowing the price of the book without asking. "No matter, you paid the ferry fare anyway, and I'll work you extra hard to make up for the difference," he said with a laugh, then added, "You have a good thing here in this book. I could have used it myself when I was trying so hard to learn. Keep it by you always, if you continue to work with plants."

Adam did not know whether he wanted to continue to work with plants. With his grandfather out of the picture he had no plans for his future other than escaping constables who might be after him. He was a rudderless boat drifting on the tide. He refused to think about it, and left such problems vaguely for later. The work he did interested him, and he liked living at Crossroads House on Fork-ed Road. That was enough for now.

The summer was hot and dry, then humid and wet, then hot and humid with slime-encrusted puddles standing from sudden rains, and bloodsucking insects rising in clouds from their surfaces. There was much sickness in the pine barrens. Dr. Micah said he had never seen so much. From time to time Adam accompanied him on his rounds, or on an emergency call. It was terrible to see so many down with swamp fever, and it was especially hard on little children. The doctor told him that no more than half the babies survived to the age of five.

"Yet that is not many more than the number of those who die each summer everywhere," he said. "Someday, Adam, I think doctors will be able to save more children."

Adam went along with the doctor to Sundew Creek to visit Jacob, whose leg Dr. Micah had had to amputate.

"Sometimes I can hardly bear the weight of the trust my patients put in me, Adam," said Micah with an unusual somberness. "I should have been able to save that leg."

"You can't blame yourself. Jacob was alone and he got up to go to work too soon. Saving his life was touch and go."

"Yes — maybe I should not set blame on myself. Yet I do."

And when they found Jacob sitting under a tree whittling on a stick the doctor was as calm and cheerful as always. Somehow he was able to leave a patient with more confidence and hopefulness, and he gave the old man a promise that he would get him a wooden leg.

On the ride home the doctor said, "Adam, if I give you

the measurements, and make a little drawing, think you can carve one out for him?"

"Aye, I believe so."

"Then take all of your time and do it. We've got to have that old chap on two feet soon, even if one is a peg. He's not the kind who can sit around doing nothing — he would soon die that way."

When he had done the job to Dr. Micah's satisfaction, and Jacob was about again getting used to his new leg, Adam went back to the barrens to strip needles from pine boughs. The pharmacist would buy as much as Dr. Micah could send him of the invigorating pine tonic, and sassafras tea was in demand, also. When Adam wasn't gathering pine needles he was digging. One day, as he chopped and stripped boughs, Adam realized suddenly how much at home he was in these woods.

They were not beautiful forests these — and not gentle; they were tough and enduring, as tough and enduring as a man had to be to live among the barrens and bogs. He looked down at the old deerskin gloves kept for this work, at stains and sticky resin on them, and remembered with a smile how he had gone out for needles without gloves the first time alone at this work. It had taken him many evenings of rubbing with bacon fat to get the stinging pitch from his skin. As he swung his big sack over a shoulder and trudged homeward with Job loping behind, he said to himself, "I reckon I'm a down-Jersey piney. At least for now."

After supper Adam pulled weeds from Mistress Jenkens' garden and marveled at her riot of enormous flowers, grown for beauty as well as for drying to make drugs and medicinal teas.

173

"Bess could grow things in a block of stone," remarked her husband. "I think it's a kind of magic."

"Don't you say things like that, Micah," said his wife uneasily. "It's bad luck. Old Jersey Devil might turn on us. He did sour milk in the springhouse yesterday, and that's a fact."

"Bess! That's enough of that talk. Speak of the devil makes folks mistrust their fellowmen. Before you know it some old woman will be accused of witchcraft, or somebody will declare she saw her neighbor with horns and a tail running along her fence rails, screeching like that Jersey Devil's supposed to do."

"So you say. But I know how the Jersey Devil was born. A woman didn't want more children when she already had thirteen, and she said she hoped if she had another it would be the devil himself. That next baby was born with clooven hoofs, tail, horns, and wings like a bat. Flew right up the chimney and into the pines with a screech heard to the shore and five miles out to sea! Everybody knows that is the truth."

Micah Jenkens seldom shouted — now he did. "Bess! Don't you ever say that again. You hear?"

Adam turned away and walked as fast as he could across the road to a hayfield, with Job following. They had not noticed his going. He had never heard those two so angry at each other before. It must be this bad summer, turning milk sour and good folks into snapping turtles. His chores were done for the day, anyway. A strange light lay over the field in dusky afterglow, mingling gold and purple in a melancholy shadowy shroud. Adam was not looking for healing plants to gather as he skirted the hayfield, almost ready to be cut by him in long, swinging sweeps of the scythe. He moved into the cooler dimness of the trees and found his way to the rim of a small, perfectly round pond that lay in secrecy among the pines.

Dropping down upon the piny ground he sat with his arms clasping his knees and, for once, wished himself far away — out in the western wilderness, like his father — or gone to sea on a whaling ship. Anywhere but in the heat and anger of this night. The moon came, a slender rim of sharp light, and the insects roared about him in blood frenzy. Adam stood up suddenly, broke off a switch of pine, and swiped wildly at his legs, shoulders, and neck as he strode back toward Crossroads House. Job followed, snapping at his own tormenters, yet not so bedeviled as was his less hairy companion.

Adam broke out of the forest into Fork-ed Road below the doctor's place and was starting for it in the darkness when he heard a horse approaching. He stepped to the roadside, calling to Job, and soon found himself looking up at Mr. Bollock.

"You chap come with me. I've got something to say to Dr. Micah. And some questions to ask."

Adam swung around and started to Crossroads House, Job growling low in the throat by his side, and the sheriff walking his horse behind. Mrs. Jenkens, coming in answer to knocking at the front door, stared at the sheriff and Adam, then called her husband.

"Evening, Mr. Bollock," said Dr. Micah. "What brings you out here at this time of night?"

"Two things, Doctor. But first I want to ask this chap where he was last night?"

"Why?" The doctor's tone was angry.

"Well — somebody broke in my tavern and stole a keg

of rum. Ain't no other stranger hereabouts but him — and nobody in Tallytown would do a thing like that to me — not if he values his hide."

"Sheriff," said Micah Jenkens, "Adam was here all night. That we know. So there must be somebody around who doesn't value his hide."

"Huh — well — did you know he was prowling up the road just now in the dark when I come on him?"

They said nothing. Bollock looked at Adam, then at the dog. "Scarfys swear they don't know him, this chap, but they are liars. He could be mixed up in them moonshining and smuggling operations of theirs. I'll warrant he was. This dog — he was seen with a Scarfy more than once, and it ain't natural he'd take up with anyone who wasn't part Scarfy anyway."

"Adam had no tie-up with the Scarfys, Mr. Bollock. He just happened on my trouble when he was walking on the road. He saved me from the pines robbers. That's all. As for the Scarfy dog, he just wandered off from them."

"So he was the chap rescued you. You can't know if he was in this house all last night, now can you, doctor? You don't know anything about this fellow, now do you?" He pushed his hat to the back of his head, scowling. "That dog, ugly brute he is, seems to be with this chap every time I see him. I been keeping an eye on him when I could now and again. Don't trust him. Mighty peculiar his circumstances be."

"Adam is all right, Mr. Bollock," the doctor's voice was quick and sharp. "I'll vouch for him. I told you so."

The sheriff stared at Micah and shrugged, "Well, you got no call to lie that I can see. You be too trusting, though. Doctor, the other thing I came to say is that the circuit judge will be here Monday next. I want you in Tallytown to testify against the Scarfys. And you bring along this chap. I want them Scarfys taken out of my jail and to the state confinement house. Or hanged!"

After the sheriff's departure Dr. Micah, troubled at his own deception and worried about Adam's difficulties, said, "I did tell the truth. I hope the good Lord will forgive me for not telling all of it."

Adam sat down heavily on a bench, wiping his face with his hand, pushing back his hair, sweating in the stuffy kitchen inside cheesecloth-covered windows, with clouds of insects buzzing furiously outside. His throat was too tight to let him speak.

Micah Jenkens picked up his old Bible and leafed through it until he found the passage that he wanted. He read aloud: "I returned, and saw under the sun, that the race is not to the swift, nor the battle to the strong, neither yet bread to the wise, nor yet riches to men of understanding, nor yet favor to men of skill; but time and chance happeneth to them all."

In the silence following the reading of the passage Dr. Micah spoke. "We trust you, Adam."

Adam swallowed. "Aye, sir, I know. I thankee."

As he stumbled up to bed he had a sick feeling in his stomach, and knew he must tell them he was wanted for murder, or start running again — or maybe both.

Chapter 18

No one talked much next day. A melancholy had settled over them, and even Bess Jenkens was withdrawn into her own thoughts. Heat increased until it sapped the spirit and took the appetite. At dusk Adam moved toward the house slowly, thankful that his day's work was done, yet slow to go in, for he had not yet told them. Job was unaccountably restless. After supper the dog kept getting up and hopping to the door, sniffing at the crack, then moving slowly back to stretch out at Adam's feet. The kitchen was stifling behind cheesecloth and closed door, yet they preferred near suffocation to being eaten alive.

"Never saw those skeeters so bad before. And big, too. Old woman I talked to in Tallytown yesterday said she saw one Jersey skeeter carry away a whole iron kettle of rabbit stew. I believe her myself. Only August now and I don't see how we'll endure till frost." She mopped her streaming face with a towel, for she felt the heat even more than the men did.

"And so much sickness," said the herb healer. "Yesterday I treated a man who said there's a peculiar kind of swamp fever in Bogquake. Different from our swamp fever here. Seems a sailor from some foreign ship mired up on the mud in Sleeping River got taken with it while he was in Bearshead Tavern — or he collapsed with it there, anyhow. He died that night in the tavern. Next day a sailor, who had been with him in town and stayed, got it and he passed away, too. His mates speak some kind of talk nobody understands but them."

"Has the sickness spread? Why do you call it different from swamp fever around here?"

"Peculiar kind. This man told me the sailors turned yellow as dandelions. That schooner brought in sugar from the West Indian islands, discharged cargo on the coast, and then sailed up the river to pick up a load of iron hollowware to take back overseas. She stuck on a mud bank across from the town. I guess that foreign captain didn't know how low the water is now."

Job pulled himself to his feet, braced his legs, and growled. He went to the door, lifted his head, and began to bark. Adam grasped him by his neck hair and pulled him down, shouting, "You're plumb crazy tonight. Nobody's out there. You stop your fuss!"

The Jenkenses went to bed early, thinking that upstairs it might be a mite cooler. Adam let Job out for a run and slipped out behind him. He felt a vague alarm at the dog's behavior and wondered if the sheriff was prowling about. Then he shook himself in disgust. Was he going lunatic also?

If Bollock wanted to take me in, and had proof of anything, he would come to the door and get me in plain daylight, he thought. Just the same he felt uncomfortable and followed Job cautiously. The dog led him around to the shed where the still was housed and stopped growling. Adam flung the door open and looked inside at bright moonlight slanting through the opening. Nothing there. He shrugged, saying with some annoyance, "Job, you really are going daft."

And yet Adam followed again when the dog ran behind the woodpile as if hunting a scent of some kind, all the while giving out low, suspicious sounds. Perhaps it was a hungry panther, or a bear? Berries had been scarce this season, Mrs. Jenkens had said, because they shriveled on the bushes in the barrens before they turned ripe. He murmured, "Dog, since you've forgotten those Scarfys you've come on so bold I don't know you anymore."

Finding nothing, Adam called out, "Time to go in, boy." He whistled for Job, who went into another fit of baying and barking that was so violent that he fell over sideways and picked himself up to bay again. A horse came up the road rapidly and stopped in the entrance to the farmyard. Then came a rapid knocking. The farm dogs raced to join the chorus. Adam grabbed for Job with both hands and shouted at the other dogs, "Stop that noise!"

They subsided. He listened, holding on to Job. Then he heard the front door slam. Immediately the newcomer and Dr. Micah came out again and Adam caught the low, carrying voice of the doctor, "I'll send word back soon, Bess."

He heard Micah go into the barn, and debated whether he should offer a hand with hitching up the buggy. Then he decided not. This was probably Henry Jenkens coming for his brother, and Adam must stay out of their private life. The buggy and the horseman left. In the silence Job barked. Adam dragged the dog into the barn, and the other dogs followed.

"I'll shut you in here tonight, Job. I think you've gone loony."

And yet as he left the barn, closing the doors securely, he stopped to listen. It was not at all like Job to act that way. Adam tried to convince himself that the dog's behavior was only his usual announcement of the approach of a stranger coming for the doctor — then he remembered that Job's uneasiness had started in the house long before the horseman had been near. Adam walked toward the light of the kitchen lamp shining dimly through its covering. Something, he knew not what, made him turn his head toward the dark fringe of pines to his left, just beyond the still shed.

Then he saw him! He was coming toward Adam like a menacing shadow. Moonlight fell on a stocky figure. Boots made a cracking on dried earth. As he strode forward he reached up to push back his seaman's cap. Adam was close enough to see the dipped eyelid.

"Adam Quinn! I want a word with you."

Adam lunged at Garf.

"Now, hold on there. I —" Garf broke off as Adam's fist struck his shoulder, sending him backward. He dodged the next blow, shouting, "Wanted to catch you alone —"

With one hand Adam grasped Garf by his jacket as he hit out with the other. The blow caught the older man in the stomach. He grunted and dodged the next one, and then, swearing, he came forward with a mighty swing that sent Adam spinning. They grappled and fought and Adam landed hard on his knees. He was up and at Garf again. Garf grasped him in a hold like a vise. Adam twisted around, sprang out of the other's grip and let go with a blow like a battering ram. Garf fell on his back, head cracking hard. Adam heard Mistress Jenkens screaming, "Adam! Stop! You'll kill him."

Blood was running into one of his eyes from a cut on his forehead. He was standing, legs braced, head forward. He looked down and saw her kneeling beside Garf. Slowly, stiffly she got to her feet. Adam's whole body let go and he stumbled, staggering backward a few steps, nearly collapsed. He was dizzy and sick, and she had to repeat herself before he understood her words, "Adam! You all right?"

He nodded and mumbled, "All right."

"Then take his shoulders. This man's unconscious. We've got to get him inside."

As they carried Garf Adam was aware of the dogs barking in a frenzy in the barn, with Job's mighty bay above all the rest. Mrs. Jenkens was chattering, unaware of the meaning of her own words. "My Lord-a-mercy, all this blood and battle and Micah gone — what'll I do? Adam —"

She stood still and stared at him, suddenly calm and very angry. "You got any sense at all? Go wash your

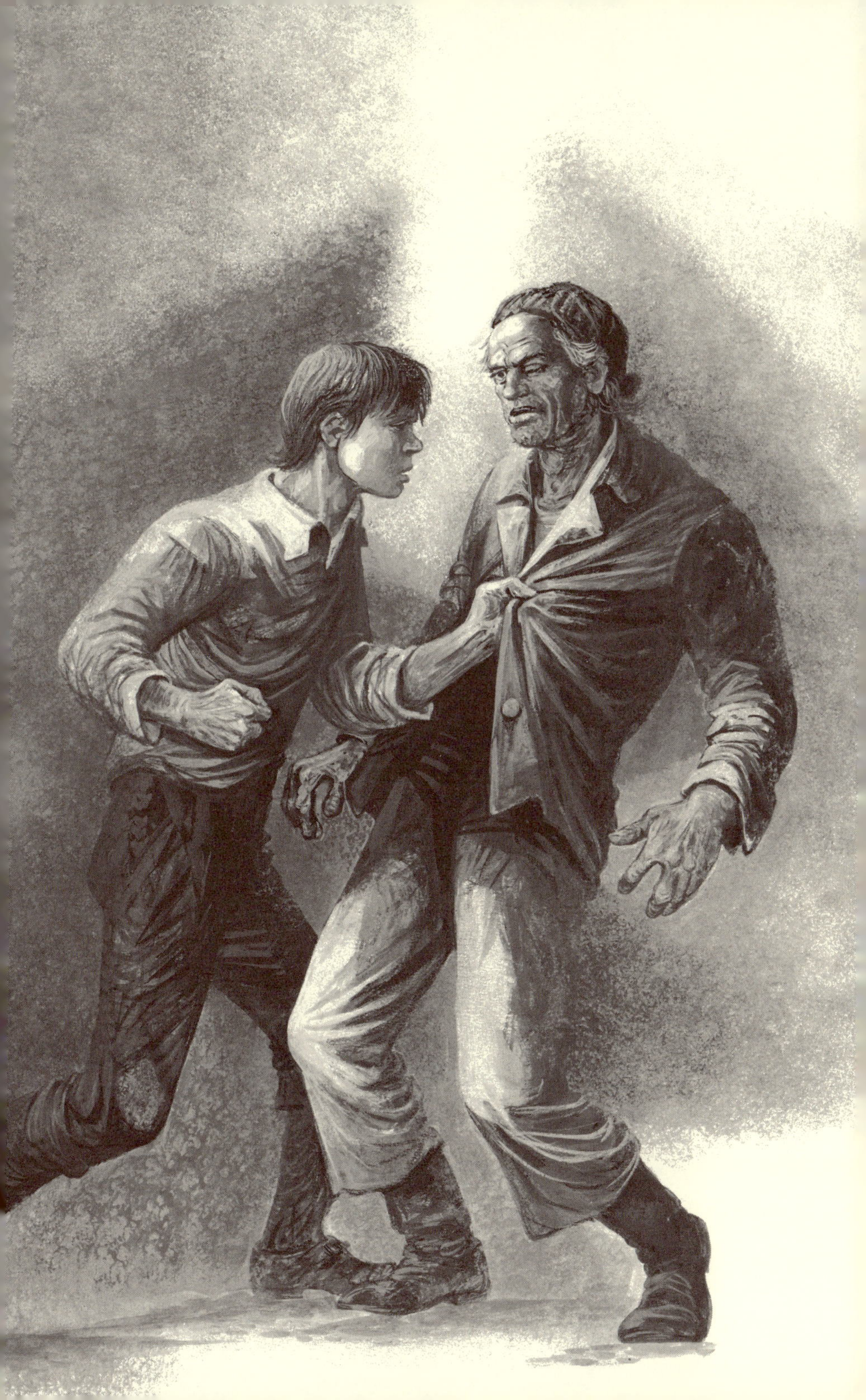

face and head and bring me water for this man. I think he's coming around now."

He stumbled out to the pump, came back dripping, with swaying bucket sloshing water on the floor. He set it down. Mrs. Jenkens, ready with bandages, salve, and rage, applied all of them to Adam.

"You got any more wounds but this head, you fool boy?" she finished off.

He shook his head dumbly and walked out of the kitchen toward the stairway. She came running after him.

"No, you don't. You don't go yet. You tell me what's this all about? Now, you tell me!"

His voice sounded hoarse and strange, "I killed him, didn't I?"

"Nonsense. He's knocked out, but his heart's pumping away all right. Pulse's not bad. He'll come to in a few minutes. Who is he?"

He told her as if it no longer mattered, as if nothing mattered anymore. "He's a constable from Philadelphia. After me this long time. For a murderous crime I didn't do on purpose."

"If you didn't do it on purpose, what for are you beating him up?"

"I can't prove it. I'll hang for it."

"Oh — yes — I see." She knew far too much of the injustice of life to need ask what he meant.

"I'll go now, Mistress Jenkens." Adam moved to the stairs to get his old knapsack and few clothes. She said, "Adam, Micah's gone — but he left a message for you."

"I heard someone come for him. I must go. I've got to get away from here now. That sheriff — he's looking for something to prove I'm a bad 'un. I've got to go away from here now. This time far away from the pine barrens."

"Why? You fixed that chap so he can't chase you tonight. I think one arm is broken. Don't know yet whether there's more, but I don't think so. I'll splint him up after you go. That message is for you. Micah wants you to go to Bogquake in the morning. Something terrible is happening there. Swamp fever's all through the town. It's the bad kind that turns people yellow. Not the usual fevers. We never had yellow fever here before, though they have had some bad epidemics in Philadelphia. Micah says he needs you. So do your friends, the Hobsons — they're both very sick."

Adam sank down on the bottom step as if his sore legs could not hold him up. He put his arms across his knees and his head on his arms. She stood silently looking down at him. Then she said, "What will you do, Adam?"

His head came up. Slowly he got onto his feet until he was looking down at her. His voice was very low, and words came painfully.

"Micah needs me? My friends need me?" He drew in a deep breath and let it out in a gasp, mumbling, "They and you, are the only friends I ever had. Took me into their home, taught me to read — " he swallowed, unable to mention Tranquility by name. "I'm going to Bogquake. Right now."

She nodded vigorously, smiling. "That's what I thought you would say. Now — don't you worry about that chap in there. I'll keep him here long as I can, with his arm healing. When I can't keep him longer I'll let him worm it out of me where you went."

"You — you'll tell him?"

"I'll tell him all right. I will. I'll tell him I promised not to let on to nobody at all that Adam Quinn told me he is making for Egg Harbor to sign on with a whaler that's in port. There's always a whaler at Egg Harbor, or one just left, or coming in. I'll say you're going round the Horn, and the Lord knows where else, for years. I'll let him worm it out of me, slow and easy-like. I don't hold with telling lies, and Micah will fault me for it, but I don't think he would hold with you hanging, either, Adam — so I'll take my chances when I tell him." She made a wry face, then chuckled, and Adam tried to smile, although his swollen mouth made it impossible.

"You take the wagon and Jehosophat. Micah went off lickety-split in the buggy."

"I won't take the wagon rig. You may need it. I'll walk."

"No — you take it. Come I need to go help Micah I'll get somebody to drive me. There's plenty that would. You can't walk that far."

"You'd be surprised at how fast and how far my legs can carry me, Mistress Jenkens. I'll just fetch my things and my dog, and go."

He gave her a sudden bear hug, then made off up the stairs, to the barn, and on out into the night.

Chapter 19

THIS WAS A NIGHTMARE of a night — moonlight gone, wind up, rain slanting down in a nor'easter from the Atlantic Ocean. Noises grew as Adam approached a wide cedar bog until the wind set up the Jersey Devil's own frolic among the trees. Tallytown looked like a deserted village, ghostly and grim under a huge buttonwood thrashing in the gale. Adam ducked his head into the wind and Job followed at his heels.

Dawn came with the storm lessening and a faint pink sky promising better things. A slow clop of a horse and a creaking of wheels made Adam cautiously seek the side of the road. The vehicle was turning into the main road from a westward fork. Was there something familiar about the gait of the horse just barely visible in early

187

light? And the shape of that wagon? Adam jumped into the road from a screen of bushes, shouting, "Ho, Kip! Hold there, Kip!"

Old Hendrickje jerked her head up in alarm. A voice bellowed, "Who's there? Who in the name of all that's decent comes jumping at me?"

"Kip! It's Adam."

"Adam? Or is it a ghostie from the bogs?"

Adam climbed in beside the driver, who thumped him on the shoulder and greeted him with enthusiasm.

"Kip, glad is scarce the word for the way I feel! What are you doing out here in the pines? I thought your route was along the Delaware, more or less."

Before he could reply Job sprang up barking as if he feared desertion. Adam reached down and pulled him into the wagon foot.

"Does that schussel of a dog go with us?"

"Aye. Job goes where I go. We're two of a kind," said Adam with a grin.

"So! An insult to you, my lad. So be it, if you say so. Now tell me, Adam, are you on your way to Bogquake?"

Adam began to talk. Why it was he did not know, but he could talk to Kip more freely than to anyone else he had ever known. He spoke of his escape through the barrens, of his rescue of the doctor, and of his life at Crossroads House. If Kip noticed that he gave no reason for his sudden flight from Bogquake he did not comment on it.

"I thought you would be far from here on your rounds by now, Kip."

"So did I. I was on my way through farmland beyond the pines when a stage coming through Widowville brought word of yellow plague in Bogquake."

Adam glanced at Kip's outline against brightening daylight and thought he had never seen his friend so sober.

"For whatever reason I know not, but it is spreading like a brush fire in the town." He turned to get a better look at Adam's battered face, and whistled, "What of you, my laddie? Why is your eye blackened? Your face is swollen and your knuckles raw."

Adam had said nothing of his fight with Garf, since he had never told Kip of his crime. He unclenched his fists slowly and spread his hands on his knees. As he did so he discovered that now, for the first time, he could speak of it. He was no longer running away. Speaking slowly, he told Kip of the visit to the Jervis office, of leaving Bolt Sherman's house, of his master's death, and of the pursuit by the bounty hunting constable. Relief spread through him as he talked, and at last, in wonder, he said, "Kip — somehow — it is strange, but when I stopped running away and determined to come back to Bogquake I felt as if a fire had burned out all my fury. I'm hoping I didn't hurt that constable much. Mistress Jenkins said I didn't. I think she would know."

He looked at the trees on either side of the road and at the white sandy strip ahead. "I don't think blind rage will ever overcome me again. Something is different."

Kip did not look at Adam, saying only. "I'm relieved to hear that, lad. How do you know that man is a constable?"

"Who else would search me out like as if he were a bloodhound hunting down a runaway slave? I think he is the man you gave a ride to last year, for his looks are odd, with those eyes, and you described him exactly."

"Aye, I remember that fellow. He's not easy to forget. And I did think him a constable at the time. Those men are paid their bounty for each culprit brought in. They do not give up easily. Only older, tough men, often as not off the sea, will do that sort of job. You have a price on your head. Aye — he's a constable."

Silence fell between them and Adam dozed off in utter weariness, awakening only when they came to the turnoff to Bogquake. Noise of wagon, cart, and horses were all about him. He opened his eyes, got his sore, stiff body straightened up, and stared.

They were facing a throng of excited, pushing people hurrying along, whipping up their horses, shouting angrily as they tried to pass. Kip said nothing, but his bushy brows were down over eyes that glared at the headlong crowd leaving town. It took them a long time to get past the straggling refugees. Several times some fellow swore at them, but Kit jutted out his chin and urged the mare on. At last they passed the stragglers and saw the furnace stack on the hill and the shining slag on the main street. Silence told them that work had stopped.

Kip spoke sadly, "Pack of cowards those are. Many a tale I have heard of the rush out of Philadelphia during the big yellow fever epidemics of 1793 and '98. Now we know how shameful a sight it is. On my way as I pass near Woodstown I've noted a tombstone placed by the family of one Major Christian Pircy, who died alone by the roadside as he fled from the city by stagecoach. It reads: "'Stay, Passenger, see where I lie, as you are now so once was I, as I am now so you must be, prepare for Death and follow me.' They do not always escape by fleeing, if they only knew it."

"How low the river is," said Adam. "And look — there's the foreign schooner."

The ship was tipped over, stuck fast in the mud, with her figurehead of a woman in flowing robes, arms uplifted, gazing down into shallow water as if aghast at her plight. INFANTA was painted in gold letters on the ship's stern. As they rode slowly along the street, the old mare too weary to move faster, they noted that nearly every house had shuttered windows.

"People in this town must be suffocating inside their homes," said Kip. "Those that have not yet run away in panic."

And as they passed by stagnant puddles from rains that had not brought relief from heat but only turned the earth into a steaming cauldron, Kip muttered, slapping at swarming insects, "A better season for pests than for men."

The church bell began a slow dirge. A funeral procession was approaching. Kip turned his horse to the side of the road and drew the wagon to a halt. Following a hearse with nodding black plumes, Mr. Edwards was a solitary passenger in his carriage. His huge bulk seemed to sink with the weight of his office, as his hands clasped a Bible. He was the magistrate of the iron town, and in the absence of a minister, he would read the last service for the dead. Kip leaned forward to call out softly to one of the men who walked behind the hearse, "Jim Bullitt, who is being mourned?"

"Jeff Turner, Mr. Kip. He's one of many buried these last few days. Yet one we all mourn."

Adam pulled on a lock of hair falling over his eye. As he pushed it back again he felt a wave of shock come over him. He found it hard to believe that a man so tall and strong and in his prime of life could be struck down. Fear rose in him. What of Tranquility? Was she still in Bogquake? If so, was she ill? He cried out, "Hurry! We must get to the Hobsons."

Kip tried to persuade Hendrickje to make more speed, and failed. Still, they were headed that way and moving steadily. As they passed Friends Meeting House Adam looked hard at it, hoping to catch a glimpse of the teacher, but it was closed and silent.

The Hobson home was, at least, alive. A horse and buggy were standing before the door. Adam leaped down, calling fiercely to Job to keep quiet. Kip unlimbered his long legs more slowly, as if quite suddenly he felt age in his knees. He followed Adam to the door, standing open to the windless heat and buzzing insects. Inside, the main room was cooler and orderly, as always, yet it had the smell of sickness. This struck them both to such a degree that neither called out, and Kip went up the steep stairs quickly with Adam just behind him, dreading what they were afraid of finding.

Voices came from a bedroom. They stood in the open doorway looking at a bed where a gaunt skeleton of a man lay, yellow as egg yolk, eyes closed, face spotted with small red swellings like mosquito bites. A stout man in black clothing bent over the bedside, holding the patient's wrist in one hand and a huge gold watch in the other. Beside the bed the town barber, also known as surgeon, was bleeding Mr. Hobson into a big bowl beside the bed. Adam's eyes turned away, sickened, and yet his heart gave a great leap. Tranquility was standing back from the bed, face white as the sheets, but, thank God, thought Adam — not yellow. She turned and at the sight of them a smile broke over her face. Kip beckoned her to the hall. The three moved downstairs to the main room.

Adam saw that Tranquility was very thin, her eyes deep wells sunk in her face. Kip put his long arm about her shoulders.

"Sit you down, lass. You look as if you need to. And tell us of this calamity that has struck the town."

"Ah, Mr. Kip — how very thankful I am to see thee. And Adam — Adam Quinn! Where did thee come from?"

"I came to help Dr. Micah. Mr. Hobson looks very low. Is Mistress Hobson — is she — ?"

"She is living, and not so ill as he is. I have been trying to care for both, not allowing my mother to come in here again. She was with Mistress Hobson at first. My mother has not been so well of late. She had fainting spells a few months ago. She is at the farm, where she has promised me to stay."

"That's good. You look as if you should be there, too, my gentle girl, so why not join your parents tonight?" asked Kip. "Adam can drive you out in my wagon. I will care for our friends the Hobsons. Don't think I don't know how, for I brought my brother out of a siege of yellow fever once, some years ago, and now he is a famous medical man in Philadelphia — and a Quaker as well. First tell us how things are here and how bad the fever rages? And how much it has spread? Do you know whether Philadelphia has felt it, too?"

"No," said Tranquility, thrusting out her chin in her old, determined way. "No, Mr. Kip. My parents are all right, I think, so long as they remain at the farm. I am staying here. As for this town — it is in grievous sorrow. So many have died since the two sailors came ashore with the plague.

"I know not much about sickness in the city, but believe

193

there is not more than the usual autumn fevers. End of summer is always sickly, as thee knows well. Yet there may be some yellow fever, so many have fled that they may have carried it with them."

"You don't look well yourself, Tranquility. You are as pale and thin as a ghost."

"I am well enough, Mr. Kip. I am weary, that is all. I must go now to assist Dr. Wellfleet and the surgeon-barber."

"Is Wellfleet bleeding people often? Hobson looks as if every drop of life in his body has been taken away."

"Yes, Dr. Wellfleet believes in heavy bleeding and heavy purging with mercury. Is not this the way to cure the plague, Mr. Kip? All say so hereabouts."

Suddenly Adam spoke, "I thought you would be gone from here before now, Tranquility. I thought you to be beyond the mountains with the mission."

She looked down, folding and unfolding a piece of her gray skirt. "They were to send for me soon, perhaps this month. But then I received word last week that the journey has been delayed until late autumn. I am ready to go when sent for, Adam."

She rose suddenly and started up the stairs, saying over her shoulder, "I must see to Mistress Hobson now."

Kip followed with long strides. "And I will see to Mr. Hobson, Tranquility. That will be my job until the Hobsons are out of danger. Adam, go look for the good herb doctor, who needs you."

At that moment Dr. Wellfleet and the surgeon-barber walked down. The doctor said to Tranquility, who came from another room to lean over the railing upstairs, "Mistress Willowby, the bleeder will return tonight to repeat the treatment. Now see here — I will leave you the calomel tablets. Massive doses of this mercury are required to save these good folks. Massive! You will not fail to see to this."

As she came down and took the pills in her hands Kip spoke up, "Dr. Wellfleet, have you no common sense at all? Taking so much blood from such a sick man will kill him — as for that calomel, all it does in such quantity is make the teeth drop out, the tongue turn black, and the body shudder into the grave."

Wellfleet's face turned purple. "Sir! I do not know who you are but think you to be some kind of mountebank in those clothes. Go back to your raree show and leave medical treatments to medical men. As for my treatment, we have the great and heroic Dr. Benjamin Rush himself to thank for this prescription. He brought the city of Philadelphia out of many epidemics of yellow fever, and with this very treatment. All qualified medical men bleed and purge. Let me pass! I am needed all over this stricken town, and I am staying here against the express wishes of my wife. I stay only for humanity's sake."

"Be that as it may, doctor," said Kip, both long arms across the doorway barring the doctor's way and forcing him to stay and listen, "I do know more than you think about medicine, and my knowledge comes not from a raree show, neither. Some physicians bleed, and some do not. The great Dr. Rush was a marvelous physician and teacher — yet he became so infatuated with his deadly bleed and purge he lost all sense about it. Who knows how many more he killed than cured, for all his courage?"

"Out of my way, fellow! Out of my way!"

"Mr. Kip, let the doctor go. Please!" begged Tranquility.

"As you say, my gentle friend. By my courtesy, doctor, so that you may further decimate the population in this calamitous town."

When the physician had left, and his barber with him, sputtering all the way out, Tranquility said wearily, "We had such trouble getting Dr. Wellfleet to come, Kip. Now he may not return. He is so busy. I could secure his services only by asking Mr. Edwards to request him to come. And Mistress Wellfleet is trying hard to persuade him to leave town."

"Good riddance, Tranquility," responded Kip cheerfully. "Now we will see if we can do better for the Hobsons ourselves. Adam, if you are still there — get Dr. Micah here at once, if you can?"

Adam went, hearing Kip calling after him from upstairs, "Take the wagon. And hurry! Hobson looks very bad. I think he's unconscious."

Adam soon found Micah Jenkens. The familiar old buggy was moving up the street faster than was usual. Dr. Micah pulled in his horse.

"Glad to see you, Adam. I can use you. There be nobody in this town and all the countryside around and about to do doctoring but Dr. Wellfleet and me. I just sent word to Bess to dispatch me more supplies by a boy from Tallytown, but not to come herself. You come with me. I'm on my way to the miller's. His whole family's down with fever, six children along with man and wife." Even as he prepared to drive off, several people came running to beg him to accompany them.

Adam called out, "Wait! Kip sent me to fetch you. The Hobsons are very bad. Dr. Wellfleet's been there just now.

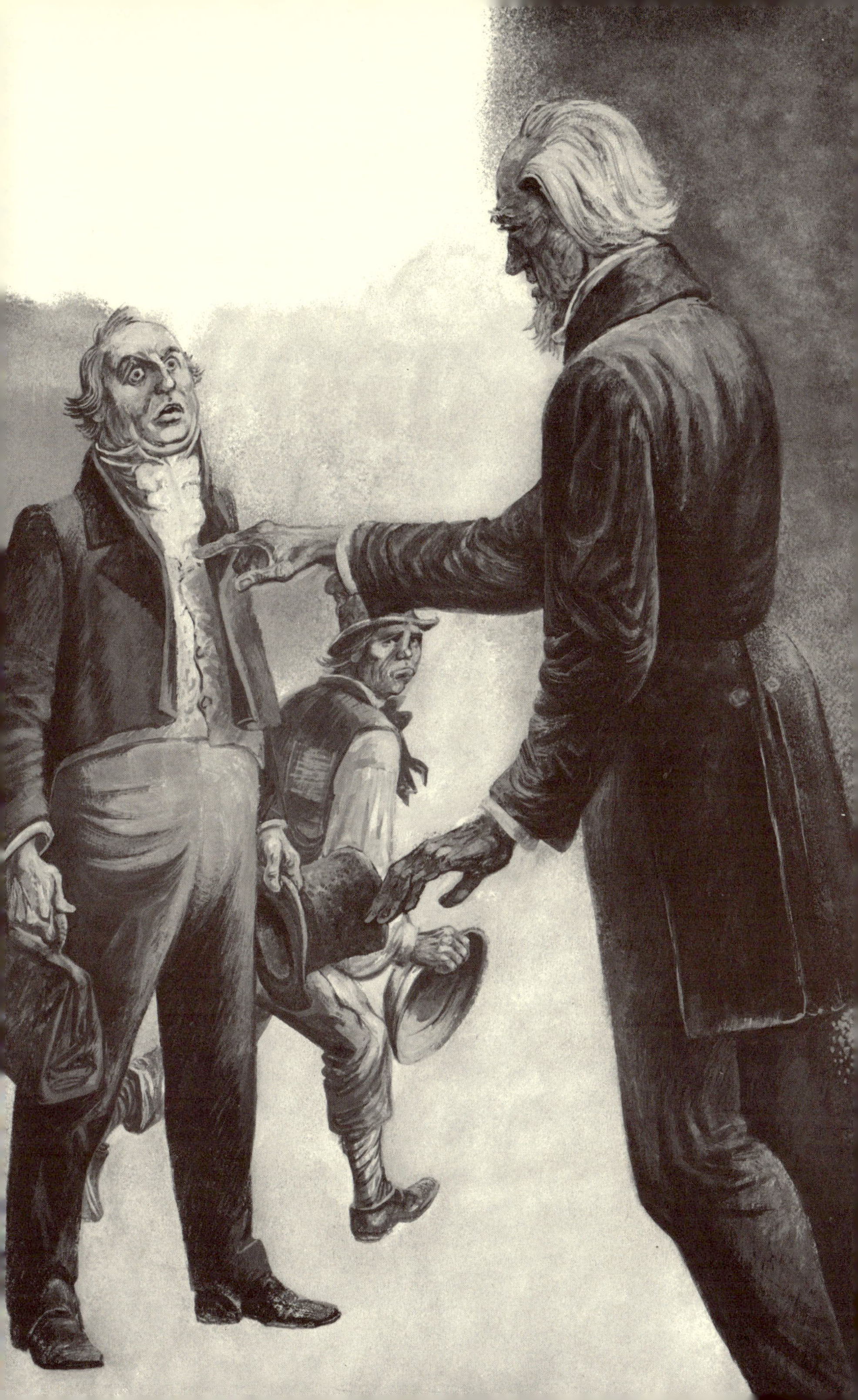

He's been bleeding Mr. Hobson heavily, and purging with mercury. Kip says that'll kill Mr. Hobson."

Micah drew in his horse again sat silently thinking, then said, "Adam, I don't interfere with medical men. I go only when I'm asked for by the sick or their kin. And not when certified doctors are already there. You go back to your friends and do what you can for them. If they can spare you, you'll find me at the miller's, or somewhere else in town. I'm not hard to locate." He smiled, nodded, and drove away.

Adam found that against Kip's advice Tranquility had sent for Dr. Wellfleet again. The physician had come, ignoring Kip as if he were no other than one of the stinging mosquitoes plaguing everybody. As Adam started for the stairs the doctor came down, patting a weeping Tranquility on the shoulder.

" 'Tis the will of God, Miss Willowby. He will comfort the afflicted."

He left rapidly, and Adam did not need to ask any questions. That same afternoon he followed the hearse to the Quaker cemetery, where new graves were fresh all around the simple markers, and he knew it was the same in the Methodist graveyard. Burials took place with haste. Mourners hurried home to care for more sick, or to be taken care of themselves. And all the while the bell tolled.

Tranquility, caring for Mrs. Hobson, drew a sighing breath as she said that her patient was a little better, but the crisis would probably be reached that night. While Kip sat with the sick woman, promising to call Tranquility if any change took place, she went to the kitchen to prepare soup and bread for the three of them. Adam, awkwardly trying to help, dropped a cup and shattered it, then spilled a basin of water, then stumbled and nearly tipped over a lamp just lit in the growing dusk of evening. At last, having held her tongue so long, Tranquility turned to say, "Adam Quinn, thee is a bull in a china shop! Never did I see such an ungainly creature, except perhaps that ugly, smelly dog you have. He looks as if every part of him came from a different kind of animal. And will thee kindly put him outside?"

Adam, face a sunset hue, grabbed Job and hauled him out of doors, sternly admonished him to stay there and keep quiet, then closed the door on growls and protests. Yet Adam was happier to hear Tranquility sounding like herself for the first time since he had arrived. As she ate a little she even smiled when he tried to tell her about Job and the strange habits and situations that dog could get into. Saying nothing, Tranquility took out a dish of scraps for Adam's homely companion. Both Adam and Tranquility were trying desperately not to think of the loss of Walter Hobson, and of his wife so ill above stairs.

That night tension eased, for Mistress Hobson grew so much better that they began to believe she would live, after all. There was one time when Rawson, the barber, came back with his bowl and lancet, and Kip, without consulting Tranquility, heard him in time to meet him at the door.

"Dr. Wellfleet sent me to bleed Mistress Hobson." The man looked scared as a rabbit.

"Ah, yes, but the good doctor does not know that I have already taken care of the patient. Yes — yes indeed. You may go and tell the physician that everything has been done, and the patient is doing well."

None of the three went to bed that night, although

Adam, creeping up the stairs at dawn, saw Mrs. Hobson sleeping, her breathing regular, face discolored but not appearing feverish, and her nurse sleeping sitting in her chair.

Before he could go down again a horse galloped to the door and a farm boy thrust his head in, shouting, "Miss Tranquility, come quick! I'm sent for you. Your ma's took very bad."

"Shut up, you dummkopf!" roared Kip, then in lower tones, "not so loud." But Tranquility was already running down the stairs. More clatter on the road and a carriage drew up. Out of it came the ironmaster's wife, and along with her a servant. The Edwards children had been sent to the shore, but their mother refused to go.

"Tranquility, my dear, Mr. Edwards has just heard from Dr. Wellfleet of your mother's illness. Go to her at once. The doctor is already there. How is Mrs. Hobson?"

Kip answered, "She is better and I believe she will live. She is over the crisis, but must not risk getting up too soon and having a remission. Someone must take care of her."

"Yes, I know. I have brought Angela to look after her. Poor woman, does she know of her loss? And a fine man he was, too. Mr. Kip, can you take Miss Willowby to her home?"

"Yes, at once." Turning to Tranquility, "Hurry, my child. Adam, help her get her bonnet and things."

Then Kip said to Adam, in a voice too low for the others to hear. "We must arrive before that doctor puts her mother too far under his treatment. Ah — if I could only get old Charles here! But long ago he made a rule not to leave the city. All I can hope for is that we push Wellfleet out of the farmhouse before it is too late."

Chapter 20

It was already too late. Tranquility flung her arms about her father, then rushed upstairs to her mother. Dr. Wellfleet was taking leave of Zack when the three of them burst into the house.

"Mr. Willowby, your good wife will be up and around soon, of that I can assure you. I will return every day and the surgeon-barber will be with me."

The barber was backing away from Kip, who stood in the front door with Adam just behind him. Rawson, his tools in hand, looked wildly about, saw the back door and went through it with remarkable speed. They heard his horse retreating rapidly.

"Mr. Willowby," said Kip urgently, "this medical man's

treatment is far more likely to kill than cure. Do not let him return."

"Sir!" bellowed the doctor, blood rushing to his face, "why do you pursue me from house to house with these lies? Get out of my way, sir, or I will horsewhip you myself!"

Kip grinned at the thought, then sobered. "Adam — go and fetch Micah. See that he comes."

"That quack! That Indian medicine man? He should be cast into prison for practicing medicine without a license, and I will see to it that he is. He murders my patients."

"Ah," Kip's voice was razor sharp. "So you say. At worst Micah's herbs do not harm. At best they help a great deal. And he gives nature a chance. Does he withdraw life's own blood and shock the body system with mercury like an earthquake? He does not! As for you, Dr. Wellfleet — you say you pattern your outpouring of life's fluid on the heroic Dr. Rush. Dr. Rush's claim to fame does not rest on that crazy treatment of his. He is honored because he was a man of skill and great courage who loved humanity. He rallied all of the city of Philadelphia to fight the yellow plague. Yes — some of Micah's patients die. As nature wills. Yes — a few of your stronger patients do get well — in spite of you. Adam, get you going!"

Kip suddenly stepped from the doorway. Adam plucked himself from his motionless position to leap out and into the wagon. The irate physician, speechless with fury, flung himself into his buggy and whipped up his horse.

Dr. Micah came with Adam this time, driving his own rig ahead of the wagon. When Adam came into the house Micah was already upstairs with Mistress Willowby, and Kip was sitting silently in the kitchen with Zack. They sat there for some time, how long Adam did not know, but when he heard slow, unsteady steps on the stairs he knew them to be Tranquility's, and he knew without being told that her mother was dead. Micah was with her, putting her into her mother's chair, saying quietly but urgently, "Here, Adam, we must look after Miss Willowby. She is taking the fever herself, I believe."

Indeed she looked so, thought Adam in a panic, for her face, so pale that morning, was now fiery red, eyes glistening with fever. He had noticed some tiny red spots that day, and he knew by now that these swellings were believed to be an early symptom of the yellow fever.

"I'll go for Mrs. Edwards," said Adam. "She needs a woman to nurse her."

"No need for that," said Micah with a little smile, as he stood by the window. "Listen!"

A horse and wagon were rocketing into the barnyard.

"Whoa! Whoa, there, Jehosophat, you raw-boned, slab-sided son of Beelzebub!" Mistress Jenkens burst into the kitchen, calling out, "You, Micah! Why did you send me a message to get a boy to come here with supplies? You think you can get away with that, do you? What do you think I am? An ornament to set on the mantel-shelf? A flower in the border patch? Here I am."

"So I see, Bess. And so I hear, too. Now be quiet! Hush. Mistress Willowby has gone to her maker but just now. And Miss Tranquility is taking the yellow sickness. Get her to bed, Bess. And take charge here. I must be off to town at once. I'll be back this evening. You know what to do as well as I do. And Bess Jenkens — don't let that barber into this house."

"Mr. Willowby," Kip turned to the old man who sat by

the stove as if stone deaf and blind, "Mr. Willowby, Tranquility is in good hands now. Let me get you to your bed."

"Leave him be, Mr. Kip," said Mrs. Jenkens gently. "It will take a piece of time before the shock wears off, and then it will be like a fresh wound, and a bad one. Best leave him there long as we can. I can look after him, too."

"I believe you can, Mistress Bess, but if you need me, or Adam, you send word by that day boy that's outside doing the farm chores. I'll attend to the burial, which must be today. Now Adam and I will do what we can in Bogquake."

Kip glanced at Adam as Mrs. Jenkens and the doctor got Tranquility up the stairs to her room. Then he took Adam by the arm with a strong grip, and shook him a little.

"You listen to me, laddie. Takes every man who can stand up to do what's to be done in that town. We'll come back here every night, and Bess Jenkens will send word by day if needed. Come with me. Doing some work will shake you loose."

Adam went with him. On the way to town he managed to pull himself in and subdue his fear, as if he sawed on the bit of a runaway horse. An atmosphere of doom seemed to have dropped down on Bogquake, and fear was visible along the street in the bonfires men made and the little piles of burning tarred rope they thought might drive out the plague. The street was hazy with acrid smoke. Men, women, and children wore small bags of asafetida around their necks and powdered sulphur dusted into their shoes. They chewed all of the garlic they could get hold of from a hawker who came through, stopped just long enough to sell out his stock of "guaranteed plague preventives," then got out of town again. Some citizens wore rags soaked in vinegar tied around their heads, and camphor added still another odor to those already making people almost too offensive to approach.

The bell clanged in their ears incessantly. As he pulled Hendrickje to a halt before the church Kip said angrily, "That bell tolling all day long and most of the night is enough to drive us all mad."

A boy let go of the bell rope and ran away, leaving behind an effluvium of garlic, asafetida, and sulphur. An old man on a slow horse stopped beside them, and the ancient Methodist parson of the pines dismounted.

"I come to Bogquake," he said, "and I find a town in anguish. The good book tells us there be a time to laugh and a time to mourn, but in a time such as this be in the town that mourning bell ought to be silenced. Don't you think so, Mr. Rembrandt Kip?"

"I do, Parson Haven. That I do. It's on your church. Then why do you have it rung all day and most of the night?"

"Have it rung? I do not. I have but just come from the barrens. The church belongs to the ironmaster. He it is who must stop it, and yet, do you not think, sir, that a rope detached might just happen by chance and save the ironmaster a problem?"

Kip winked at Adam, saying, "Well, a strong young laddie might be able to swarm up to the belfry."

Adam went to a pillar over the back porch and up it hand over hand. Reaching into the little belfry he untied the rope and jumped to the ground where he handed it to the parson, who said severely, "Mr. Kip, I do not intend to be a party to such thievery. I never said I would."

"Who wants to steal, parson? Not I. Adam, can you find a place to shove it under the church porch?"

As Adam did it, and then returned to the seat in the wagon, he looked around at sound of Dr. Micah's voice.

"I've even considered doing that job myself. There's so much to be done here I don't know what to do next. Adam — you told me once you lived in Mistress Anderson's boarding house. Go there and persuade her to take in the sick, if you can? They are coming in now from outlying places. See how they are left in wagons out in the broiling sun — for lack of beds to put them in. Many houses will not open up for them."

Adam turned to thread his way through the vehicles standing in the hot street. He had some misgivings about facing Mistress Anderson and thought it most unlikely he could persuade her to do anything at all.

Micah Jenkens called him back. "Adam, don't quarrel with Dr. Wellfleet. He is doing what he believes to be right. He can't stop me from doing what I think be right. Nobody has yet. I care nothing for being called a quack."

All the way along the street Adam saw and pitied crying children wandering about as if they knew not what to do or where to go. In this town life had slowed to near stopping. His head throbbed painfully. He shook it as if to cast off his despair. If only he had been allowed to stay at the farm where he could have watched over Tranquility! And still he knew he could do nothing for her, and she was in far better hands than his.

Adam knocked on the closed door of the workmen's boarding house. There was no answer. He knocked again. Then he opened the door and hesitantly walked to the kitchen and thrust his head inside. Mistress Anderson, skirt tucked into her belt, cap awry, was bent over a big caldron like a witch at work on a spell. She glanced around.

"So it's you again! Come back like a bad penny. Thought I disposed of you — you fire-eater."

The kitchen looked as if a high wind had swept through it, overturning kettles and pans, spreading out food helter-skelter on the tables, and flapping open cupboard doors. The range burned fiercely, and, although the room was stifling, the woman's hands moved rapidly and she was cool and collected while cutting potatoes and making soup. An enormous can of milk stood beside her on the floor.

"I came to ask if you can take in some sick people?"

"You simpleton! What do you think I am doing? Upstairs I've got three sick furnace workers, two mill men, and a bog raiser. I'm all alone here, too. All my help has run away, and I'm not made of bog iron myself, you know."

Adam had thought before now that she probably was, but all he said was, "I'll lend a hand."

All day he worked so fast and furiously that he had no time to think of Tranquility, and still his breath stuck in his throat so he could not speak when he saw Dr. Micah coming in.

"I've had word from Bess that Miss Tranquility is doing fairly well, and she's stronger than she looks — that young lady. Fever's down a little."

He continued as if he hadn't noticed the huge sigh bursting from Adam's chest. "Now, I'm come to do what I can here. I see there was no need to persuade Mistress Anderson."

Suddenly the lady herself erupted from the kitchen, "It's about time you got here, Micah Jenkens. Those men have fever burning in their stomachs. Are you going to help them or aren't you?"

Dr. Micah laughed, "Ma'am, your words scorch the air — but your deeds will put feathers on your wings in the great by-and-by. Can you take in more patients?"

"Yes. I've some empty beds in the garret, and more can be bedded on the floor if need be. But not unless I get some women to help me. This firebrand boy has been a-working like six all day. Where are all those church-going ladies of this town? Run like rats from a sinking brigantine, no doubt."

"No — not at all, ma'am. The tavern is filled with the sick, and with Quaker and Methodist ladies nursing them, even in the taproom where they never set foot before. Some of the Negroes are down sick at Sandy Run, and yet those who are well and can be spared have come in to help here. At the ironmaster's house the mistress herself is ill today, and so are some of her servants. And the place is filled with sick being nursed by townswomen. Listen! You can hear wagons coming in from the barrens."

Adam went to the window. These wagons were bad to look on. Sick were being brought in from charcoal burner camps and lumbermen's shacks, as well as from settlements and cabins deep in the pines. And with them were women and children.

How could this evil disease have spread so fast? Was it a miasma spawned in the bad air of a swamp and blown here by the wind? Was it poison bred mysteriously on board that foreign ship, then borne far away by the wind? No one knew. People took it for granted that such illnesses came on them as a judgment from God in punishment for their sins. As with the Tower of Babel, Adam thought.

Or the plagues of Egypt. Adam told himself he did not really believe that. Mercy Willowby could not have committed any sins, nor had Walter Hobson. Someday physicians would know why and how to stop a plague.

As Adam helped bring in sick men to the garret he thought of Charley Coons, who, he had heard, had been one of the first to die here. Suddenly Adam remembered catching glimpses of women's eyes peering around drawn curtains in their windows. He ran down the stairs and into the street without waiting to explain.

Slowly he walked along the rows of houses. Was that a curtain moving? Pounding on the locked door he shouted, "Open up! Open up or I'll break in the door!"

A screech reached him. He shouted again, pounding with both fists. Sound of voices and the door opened partway to disclose three pairs of frightened female eyes.

"Nobody can hide from the plague! Come with me. We need your help."

The oldest woman frowned, looking scared, but she said slowly, "Sisters, he is right. Young man, we will go along with you."

Although two of the sisters shook with fear, they all followed him to the boarding house. Mistress Anderson gave them a sour glance, saying, "All right, you're needed to nurse the sick, Emily Bolton, and so are Jane and Samanthy — if they can stop shaking."

Adam went down the street to look for Kip. He found him surrounded by frightened children. Adam picked up a small girl who was having trouble keeping up with Kip's long strides. At the Quaker Meeting House they placed the children with others in the care of two young girls.

"The children who come down ill will be taken to the

ironmaster's house, and the others will be brought in as we find them," said Kip. Then, turning to Adam, "Come along. Let us locate Edwards and discover if we can bring some order to this place."

It was easy to see how badly order was needed here; the whole town was noisome with rotting garbage and the bloated bodies of dead animals, along with smoke from barrels of burning tar and the bonfires and smoldering hemp. Walking rapidly they paused at the sound of a galloping horse. A priest drew in his mount and swung himself to the ground. He strode toward them, cassock flapping about his boots, and held out a hand to Kip, who took it in a hearty grip as a smile spread over his anxious face.

"Welcome Father, but why have you come to this desolated town?"

"I came when I heard good Catholics were being buried haphazard enough to make me skin crawl. I came to rectify that outrage. And what, may I ask, are you doing here?'"

"The same as you, I believe — for I do not think the reason you give is the only one. We are on our way now to see Mr. Edwards to discover how we can make ourselves most useful. There is big trouble here such as you have not seen before, unless you weathered the epidemics of '93 and '98 in Philadelphia."

"That I did, both of 'em, though young at the time. I know something of the panic that can demoralize a place."

"This is Adam Quinn, Father Aloysius."

"A good Catholic name if ever I heard one."

"I'm not Catholic — nor Quaker, either," said Adam with a scowl.

They turned into the drive leading to the ironstone house, and the priest tied his horse to a hitching post. He gave Adam a smile.

"Me boy, a Quinn can never be a Quaker. You look as solid an Irishman as any paddy on the streets of Cork. I'll welcome you yet into the faith of your fathers."

Priests didn't circuit ride as parsons did, and Adam remembered that to go to mass Irish workmen had to ride all the way to Burlington — and seldom did. He glanced curiously at the priest, but made no reply.

Men and women were crowding into the little office, and Mr. Edwards, his bulk overflowing his chair, was sallow and sagging. Looking at him, Adam wondered if the ironmaster was really able to be out of his bed himself. Mr. Edwards said, "Gentlemen, find chairs and be seated. I will not attempt to rise to welcome you, for I am not sure that I can, yet never have I been so glad to see newcomers in Bogquake. Father Aloysius, if you have come to bury the dead you will find plenty of work here."

"Don't rise, Mr. Edwards. You look as though you are coming down yourself, although we all hope not. I did come for that purpose, and to see that none of my people go to purgatory unshriven."

"You will stay awhile?"

"Stay I will, sir. And do what I can. I hope not to spend all of my time with the dead and the dying."

"Good. I would entertain you in my home, but it is a hospital, and there isn't a bed to spare."

"Never you mind about that. There are plenty of empty houses, I presume, for in Burlington we heard that the exodus was a rout.

"I met some on the road meself," he continued. "There

was a carriage driven by your town medical man, Wellfleet by name, I believe, and his wife jouncing alongside. I suppose it was his wife, unless he was making off to perdition with somebody else's spouse. I shouted to ask him where he was going in such haste, and he pulled in with the lady screaming, 'We aren't wanted in that town! Risked his life — got no thanks. We're going to my father's in the city.'" Father Aloysius ended with a wry look.

The ironmaster sighed, then said, "Dr. Wellfleet did work hard here. Perhaps he will return after his wife is safe in the city. And now, what can I do for you, Mr. Kip?"

"As you know, I've gathered strayed children into the Quaker Meeting House. What can I do now? Food is running low all over town, I'm told."

"Yes, I've sent two wagons to Burlington for food and medicines. Mr. Kip, perhaps you will take charge of distributing provisions when the wagons return and see that those in charge of the hospitals get medical supplies and—" He paused to greet two newcomers, who quietly pushed their way into the room. Adam stood back to let them by. He recognized Mr. Hiram Joynas, who was both manager of Matilda Furnace works and the leading Quaker of the town. With him was Parson Haven.

"Mr. Edwards," said the aged parson, rubbing his long jaw with a gnarled hand, "something must be done about cleaning up this town. Nobody bothers to convey refuse to the dump pit in the woods anymore. The town stinks, sir. And the conditions inside houses are pitiful."

"Yes." The ironmaster's huge body sagged lower in his chair. "But where do we get some who will do it, Mr. Haven? We must make do with those we have and pray they may be spared the plague. Mr. Kip, can you take charge of cleaning the streets? Parson Haven is doing yeoman service assisting Dr. Jenkens."

Adam brushed his hair back with a nervous hand and said, "I can help with that, sir."

"Very well. You are Adam Quinn, aren't you? Mr. Joynas, with few duties at the furnace now, is spending much time assisting the nurses in my home and at the tavern. There are more cases reported at Sandy Run, and we must establish a hospital there. Mr. Joynas, can you go there also and take charge?"

The Quaker picked up his broad-brimmed hat.

"Adam Quinn," continued the ironmaster, "your task is a mountainous one, but I know not where to get assistance for you in the performance of it."

"That I'll do," spoke up the priest. "I think I know where there may be a crew. I heard this plague started with the death of two Spanish sailors from the schooner yonder in river mud."

"Yes, that is so. We cannot persuade the men to come ashore now that two of their mates are dead. Only their captain speaks a little English. As far as we know none of those on board the *Infanta* are ill, yet when someone rows out to ask for assistance the men vanish below decks."

"Ah —" said Father Aloysius, "leave that to me."

As they came out of the office two wagons loaded with supplies were rolling into town. Kip strode off toward them to get the food distributed, and Adam went to look for horses and empty wagons.

Chapter 21

There was no time to think, and Adam did not want to, for when he did he fell into desperate anxiety about Tranquility. He located several idle wagons and found horses and mules, left untended and hungry in their stalls. On his way he encountered two stableboys from Bearshead Tavern who were leaving town. Roughly he grasped each by an arm saying, "If you leave Bogquake now the ironmaster will have you found and clapped behind bars. Go to every place in town, locate all animals — horses, mules, dogs, cats, chickens, and ducks — all of them! Feed and water them all. Get feed from the store. Don't you pass one by or I'll take care of you — myself!"

They scurried to do the job, eyes terrified. Adam's own

gaze was grim, and he did not worry at all that his threats were impossible to carry out, just so long as those boys believed them. He thought they would do as told now.

Adam paused to look at the long street, once shining and clean. Bogquake citizens seemed to have lost all decency and to be living in a panic. Instead of carting to the dump pit decaying vegetables, dead rats, meat left too long untended and now thrown out crawling with maggots — along with rags, boxes, and sacks of cheese rinds and rotten eggs — they were throwing it all into the streets. The sun beat down mercilessly on it. And stables and barns were befouled beyond belief.

He considered burning refuse on the numerous fires smoking along the streets and decided against it. For all he knew, that might spread the plague farther through the poisoned air. Instead, he found a shovel, piled a wagon high, and drove it into the forest to the town pit, only to find it overflowing. He went to work digging, and when the dump was enlarged a little he drove back to town in a desperate mood. Where was he to get some help to cart and bury this mountain? How could he dig more pits alone?

"Adam Quinn! Hold!"

He pulled up beside Father Aloysius and a group of sailors chattering in Spanish.

"Lucky for you it is that I spent some time schooling in Spain in me youth, for I can converse with these fellows. I did discover from the captain of the *Infanta* that he lost several of his crew to the yellow sickness and buried them at sea after leaving Barbados. Some others had it too, but recovered on the voyage."

"How did you persuade them ashore then?"

"There are ways, you know," he winked at Adam.

"Purgatory be a strong argument, and at a time like this a father must persuade his recalcitrant children by means fair or foul. Put them to work. I'll give them instructions, if you will but tell me what."

That was the beginning of a partnership between Adam and the priest. Together they went to the store and found it empty of storekeeper or assistant clerk. They took away shovels, picks, and feed for the animals. They found and lined up in the street horses, mules, and carts as well as wagons. Adam led his crew of seamen in outlandish Spanish garb up and down streets, in and out of houses, and back and forth to the pines. The priest went along on the first trip out then disappeared from time to time when called by urgent request. Adam noticed that for all his talk about infidels he always went even to Protestants when called to aid.

Climbing into the wagon after one such visit the priest said, "This is not time nor place for theological dogma. I'll say no masses over unbelievers, but I'll go when called to do what I can with word or deed. And when I get the time again I'll argue the teeth out of that parson, or the Quaker fellow, either — alone — or in tandem. Right now they do as much as you or I, and who stops for argumentation?"

Adam moved these days as if in a waking confused dream, for he got very little sleep. Nearly every night he and Kip paid a visit to the farmhouse, where Mistress Jenkens always greeted them with, "How is my Micah doing?"

They could tell her only that when they got a glimpse of him he seemed well enough. As for Tranquility, she was yellow as butter, thin, and as yet able to swallow nothing but sips of gruel and milk. Yet her nurse was unworried.

"She's got a down look, but she'll make it."

The Spanish sailors turned out to be good-natured, singing and shouting at each other, and they were good and willing workers now that they were into it. Father Aloysius, most of the time with the sick, told Adam to call him if his crew caused trouble or refused to work. There was no need, except once when a fight erupted among them, and the priest had to dodge into their midst roaring in Spanish.

Insects tortured by day and especially at night. A light rain brought no relief, but added puddles soon to dry in a baking sun. When hope was at its lowest point a shout came from the river. Those who were able to walk gathered at the wharves to stare downstream in disbelief. With the first real breeze in weeks came a fleet of rowboats. From them jumped men declaring that they had arrived ready to do what they could for the stricken town.

"Who are they?" asked Adam of Kip.

"Who but clammers from Clamtown, at the river's mouth. And Clamtown is not stricken with fever itself. This is a miracle. I'll be a schussel if it ain't!"

With their arrival a new spirit sprang up in the iron town. The coming of the clam diggers marked a turning point. Panic disappeared, and fear was pushed aside to let work take its place. Clammers assisted Kip distribute provisions, and two of them took over the wagons when the drivers came down with the sickness. Three others went out to Sandy Run to help Hiram Joynas, his wife, and three daughters, who were running a hospital in a barn there.

Dr. Micah, looking like a brother skeleton to his prized

Ben, said, at last, that the plague was on the wane.

"We have fewer cases this week than last, and last week there were not so many as the week before. More are recovering. Sound of hammer and saw is not going all day long now, with the making of pine coffins over there at the lumber mill and shop. Hope is springing up for us all with that fresh breeze from downriver."

The breeze had salt in it to taste on the tongue, and it cooled the town a little. Adam rejoiced for Tranquility, who no longer needed nursing and was able to keep house for her father.

Bess Jenkens was now living in the boarding house, nursing patients there. She also went from house to house, wherever she was needed. She said she couldn't catch the fever because she was too mean to die. Adam thought that might be the reason he had not caught it, at any rate. And Kip said he couldn't die either — not until he had seen the country where Rembrandt van Rijn had lived and painted.

Very late one night Adam was plodding toward the boarding house with no thought beyond falling to sleep on the quilts he kept for himself on the kitchen floor. Moonlight silvered the street and picked out the head of the bear on the sign before the tavern. Windows were dark in the empty taproom, but above stairs, where there were several patients, a tallow light burned. Adam turned weary eyes to the feeble glow. He was so exhausted that his head felt light as thistledown, and he had trouble recalling what he was to do on the morrow. He stumbled, shook his head to clear it, and his steps slowed.

He thought he heard a low moan. He knelt beside a huddled figure on the road. It was Dr. Micah. Adam leaned close, his own breath caught in throat as he felt for the heartbeat. The throb was there. He leaped up and ran into the tavern, shouting hoarsely, "Help me! Somebody help!"

"Who's there?"

Down the stairs stumbled the parson, collar off, his neck like a wrinkled turkey's in the light of candle held out before him. Behind him came the quick steps of a Quaker lady.

"It's Dr. Micah! He's taken with the sickness."

They carried the herb doctor inside and up the stairs, where an empty bed was found.

"I'll stay with him," said Adam. But Parson Haven, seeing Adam swaying on his feet, said sharply, "You need rest yourself, young man. The nurse and I can take charge of the doctor. There is a blanket and cot downstairs. Go and lie down, Adam."

"No. I'll stay here."

"Then go and find his wife — if you must do something. She is the one to care for him."

"Mistress Jenkins?" Why couldn't he think straight tonight? The long strain was getting to him, he realized.

"I'll go for her."

Mr. Haven said no more, but pulled up a stool and sat beside the doctor. Adam found Bess Jenkins nursing a patient at the boarding house. She listened, her face drawn, then called Mistress Anderson to take care of the man in the bed and went with Adam without another word. She was thin and quieter than he had ever seen her, he thought.

That night Adam watched her bathe her husband's face and chest with cool water and pine oil, lay a cloth wrung out in vinegar on his brow, and lift his head to take sips of water. She had not talked at all, except to ask Adam to return to the Anderson house to get her basket of medicines and some of her clothing.

Then she told him to go down and sleep on the cot. He refused. She did not argue but said he could bring up a quilt and lie on the floor if he wanted. He was ashamed to sleep, and yet he did in snatches, to awaken as tired as before.

Days and night ran together, mixed and confused, like a dream terror. Eating, doing errands, walking up and down, talking to Kip and to the parson, and the Quaker nurse — all of these took place and were not distinct in themselves to Adam. Dr. Micah's body seemed consumed in a fire raging uncontrolled. He came out of unconsciousness into delirium, and Adam's own stomach went into spasms until he had to leave the room. Through it all Mrs. Jenkens was calm, yet he knew she prayed with every breath. Kip came and went, as did Mr. Edwards, the Joynas family, and others. At last Kip took Adam firmly by the shoulders and put him down on a cot in the taproom, saying, "Adam Quinn, killing yourself will not bring Dr. Micah around. If you try to get up this night I will personally hold you down until dawn."

Adam slept that night and all of the following day, and when he awakened, feeling as if he had been drugged, he found a smiling Kip beside him, froth of white hair on end, green eyes shining like the slag road.

"Laddie, do you have the sense now to listen with two good ears? Then listen! The crisis came on the fourth night, which was last night. Dr. Micah is weak as blue milk, but he is going to live. And now, after you go up to see that I am not lying to you, will you get back to work? You are sorely missed in this town. It kreissels me, if you ain't!"

Adam took in a deep breath, expelled it suddenly, grinned, thrust back his hair and asked, "What of Mistress Jenkens?"

"She's asleep, with Quaker ladies in charge of both of the Jenkens. So off with you to the wagons. We must work awhile now. I've got a load of flour, bacon, and turnips to deliver, and no time to waste blathering with you."

As together they stepped out into dusk Adam shivered. "Am I taking the plague? I'm cold to the marrow."

"If so, then so am I. Since yesterday the weather has turned. See how the grass is frosted near the river! The chill has killed the flying stingers too, and me skin rejoices. This cool will dispose of the yellow fever, for we know that cool weather has stopped it in the past, though we know not why. Bogquake will take a new lease on life, although there are so many empty houses and so many houses with empty chairs. Grief has made this town its home. And the need for us right now is work. Zur Ehres Gottes und des Nachsten Bestes. To the glory of God and my neighbor's good."

Chapter 22

OLD RESIDENTS long away from Bogside were returning as if they had merely gone for a holiday, and they avoided speaking of the plague. Newcomers were leaving, having done what they came to do.

Adam and Kip were on their way to the forest to cut firewood. "How little we know of the reasons for plagues," remarked Kip. "And what a conglomeration of theories there are on that subject. I wonder if learned physicians will ever discover the reasons for them — and why and how they are spread? Or why cold weather stops them?"

"I've thought about it a lot," said Adam. "Learned physicians do say that air is made up of solids and gases, and a miasma mist grows in swamps to poison the atmosphere. And swamps we do have in plenty. Yet, if so, why did it come only with the two sick sailors? And there are those, like old Granny Bosworth, who declare the Jersey Devil came here and did his evil. Only last week Jim Weatherwax told me he heard the devil scream in his barnyard at midnight, and next morning found his ox dead."

"Adam, you don't believe in the Jersey Devil, do you?"

"No. Dr. Micah says there are no devils but those men make for themselves in their minds and hearts."

"He's a wise man, that herb doctor. My brother, Charles Lafitte, would brush him off as a quack and a fraud, say his medicine does no more than make a patient comfortable. Yet I believe there is more to it than that. The touch of his hand seems to put new life into a sick person."

"Aye — he told me it was the will to live that he gives them. How he does that he could not tell me — nor know himself. But look! There's Dr. Wellfleet and his lady, too."

The medical man passed them without a sign of recognition, although Kip gave the returning citizens an ironic wave of his whip. Job raised his head to growl.

"I doubt me the good man and his Frau will be greeted with much warmth in this town." He guffawed, and Job raised his head again in alarm. "I hope former patients will not run him out of town on a rail. But then, events are soon forgotten. Let a man but break a leg and he will be back with good Dr. Wellfleet — or a woman get a spell of vapors and she will call him in. And no doubt he will cure them both."

The plague was over and the whole place smelled fresh and clean once more. Asafetida, garlic, sulphur, and camphor had been discarded, and vinegar remained on the shelf and not on head rags. Some convalescents still lay in their beds, others crept to the street, faces faded to a sallow white, and the red swellings that had itched in the fever onslaught were gone. Days were cool and sunny, and nights chilly enough for a fire in the Franklin stove, or on the hearth.

"Why did some catch fever and not others, Kip?"

"It mystifies me, lad, it does indeed. Perhaps we are too ornery and worthless to attract it."

"Not you," said Adam, "As for me — aye."

The clam diggers were toasted at the tavern by the town, or rather those in the town who frequented the tavern, and the ironmaster thanked them publicly at the wharf as they jumped into their boats, saying they would be back, but next time strictly on business to sell a load of clams for chowder.

The Jenkenses had already gone home to Crossroads House, where Mrs. Jenkens had left neighbors in charge. She had departed loudly, wondering whether the place had gone up in smoke by now, until her husband had said that it was probably in better condition than they themselves had left it. Dr. Micah said to Adam, "Come back to us if you can, and if you can't we won't fault you. You have to find your way, Adam — and God go with you in the finding."

Not long after that, Father Aloysius hoisted his cassock and swung his legs over his horse with a hearty farewell, along with a firm admonishment to his true believers to get themselves to Burlington to Mass at least once a month.

"And Adam Quinn," he shouted. "A name like that belongs with us. See to it you come along!"

Adam laughed, waved, and laughed again when Job took after the horse in a short series of lolloping runs, baying loudly. Shortly after the priest had gone, Parson Haven filled his saddlebags with Methodist tracts, bread, hard cheese, tough ham, and a flask of pure water. He then climbed upon his steed, and, looking down at Adam, he drew his lips into a grimace that was probably a smile, nodded his white head, settled his strong old body into the saddle, where it fitted exactly, and declared in his singsong tone, "Out in the piny woods I tried to bring a stray lamb into the shepherd's fold. I succeeded only in filling his body with food. I failed to fill his soul with eternal light. Come ye with me, to join the church, and the good Lord will give you strength a thousandfold."

Adam grinned, thinking that this man's strength was truly a thousandfold over his bodily appearance.

"Parson Haven, Father Aloysius has just tried in vain to bring me into his fold. I must be 'a brand for the burning.'"

Tranquility came out of the store and walked over to wish the parson well on his journey. The old man, glancing at Adam's face, said with a sly grimace, "I suspect we Methodists will lose you to Friends Meeting, young man, on a day not too far away."

He called farewell to others gathering around and walked his nag out on the pine barrens road. They saw him reach into his saddlebag, withdraw a book, open it on his saddle, settle his spectacles, and begin to read.

"Now, what did he mean by that remark, Adam?" asked

Tranquility. "Thee has made it plain as plain thee will never be a member of Friends Meeting." Her eyes opened wide as she looked at him, for his face was as red as a Spanish sailor's cap.

There followed a warm spell, coming overnight, and the next day it rained, and it rained, and it rained, until Kip exclaimed, as he dried himself morosely in the tavern where he and Adam had taken shelter, "Forty days and forty nights — and our next job's to build an ark!"

Yet nobody got sick from the warm, wet spell, and when the rains stopped and the sun came forth, the whole world was fresh-washed and shining. All up and down the street people came out to stand taking deep breaths of the new air.

"No solids and gases here," said Adam. He had thought much about those theories proclaimed by knowledgeable physicians, and he now wondered about them as he had once wondered what it would be like to know how to read. He was cast down and miserable, confused and restless. He had been putting out of mind his own future, yet it troubled him. Was he to go back to Crossroads and continue as helper to the Jenkenses? He felt obligated — and still, he knew they would not want to hold him if he wished to go elsewhere. Where should he go?

He was jostled by men and boys running to the wharves. Wind was up, blowing hard. Sleeping River was awake with rushing water, and the tide was in. A great shout arose on the deck of the *Infanta*. Adam joined the throng on the wharf.

"Viva *Infanta!*"

Adam was nearly shoved into the brown water by six

sailors who came pelting down from the tavern, leaped into their small boat, and pulled for the schooner. The low, sturdy ship was slowly righting herself, rocking sideways, turning, boom swinging from side to side, coming free in the higher tide and the rain-swollen current. The lady at the prow was upright, face lifted to the sky, wooden arms outstretched, mud-spattered bosom gleaming in the sun's appreciative rays.

Across the water Adam heard the Spanish captain shouting at sailors who were doing a fandango on the forward deck. The small boat caught up with the ship and sailors swarmed over the rail. Dancing stopped abruptly as the captain exploded orders. Sailors leaped to their work. Jibsail ran up the mast. The small sail caught the wind and swung the schooner's bow downstream. The crew raised the mainsail just in time and the *Infanta* slowly straightened out. Adam saw lines slack, the wind catch and fill the mainsail; the *Infanta*, barely afloat, yet safely off the mud, began to move downriver. A shout went up from the shore. The schooner disappeared toward the wide-spreading marshes at river's mouth on her way to the sea.

As he turned to leave the dock Adam saw the ironmaster beside him. Mr. Edwards said, "Well, Adam Quinn, and so you and I are here when too many of us are gone forever. Yet Bogquake survives, and who knows whether it would have, had it not been for good friends who came to help us. Would you like to stay? So late in the year, winter coming on, means there's no point in trying to put the furnace in blast now. In the spring, if you like, you may have a job in the ironworks, or one of the mills. Or, better yet, how would you feel about taking over Jeff Turner's place as head smith? Or will you return to Crossroads House?"

Adam stared down at his boots, scuffing one of them miserably on the road. He chewed his lip, knowing that not even when he had wandered in the pine barrens like the first and only man on earth had he felt so lost and confused. Not even when he ran like a fox, dodging, turning, twisting to avoid capture. He was still a fugitive — and that he knew full well. The ironmaster glanced at him thoughtfully.

"I — sir, don't think me ungrateful," said Adam, "yet I cannot truthfully tell what I want to do."

"Take your time. You have the winter before you, if so be you wish to work at the furnace. And the smithy can wait a little, although not until spring. I hear you and Rembrandt Kip are going out to help farmer Willowby get in as much of his harvest as he has left."

"Aye — I'm meeting Kip now. He has gone for his wagon."

With Job beside him, Adam walked slowly up the street. There was no sign of Kip and his lugubrious Hendrickje. The rousing "halloo" of the stage driver's arrival struck his ears. With a crack of the whip, thud of hoofs, rattle of wheels, and shouts of passengers and onlookers, the rocking coach pulled up so abruptly before the tavern that its team reared and came down with a jolt. Adam, moving closer to the excitement, was thinking that these passengers must be about the last of the runaways returning.

Jumping down with an agility beyond his years, a fellow with one arm splinted and tied in a rag around his shoulder, took a stride toward Adam. Then he stopped. Adam could not have moved if his life depended on it, as he knew it did. The man's right eye, cold, pale, and blue was wide open. The left lid came slowly up to a slit disclosing the mismatched brown eye. For the first time in light of day Adam was staring straight into the face of Garf.

A hot wave of fear, anger, and shame swept over Adam. They stood a moment, others chattering around them. Neither spoke. Adam's mouth was dry, tongue stiff. At last he said, "I wanted to get away. Didn't mean to break your arm — you came at me in the dark —"

"It warn't no break. A crack, maybe, when I slipped. You've got ox arms, sonny, but you ain't man enough to down me if it was so I hadn't slipped my footing."

Abruptly a door swung open in Adam's mind. He no longer wanted to run. He knew why he had felt so confused and lost ever since the plague subsided, not knowing what he wanted to do. He had expected this meeting with Garf without knowing it. Perhaps he had been waiting for it.

Adam spoke stiffly, "I'm ready to go back with you. I guess I've been ready longer than I knew."

The man's sleepy lids, both drooping low, were raised to deliver a glare.

"Go with me! Not if I pick and choose my mates, and I don't pick a cove like you! Wildcats ain't in my circle of acquaintance."

"Didn't you come to take me —"

"Take you where? I wouldn't take you far's the jug tavern. Not if you offered to swill me down in brandy wine."

"Then why have you followed me? You dogged my steps everywhere I went. You hunted me like as if I was a fox."

"You ain't no fox, sonny. A mean bear cub maybe, or a stinkin' polecat. You think I couldn't have caught you up all them months had I tried? You don't know Garf, that you don't. I was put on your track by my master, Gentleman Jervis, as we used to call him in the good old days when I was black-birding on his ships. After he stopped slave running I was working for him in what you might call the smuggling trade. He put me on your trail. All he wanted was to get news of where you was, and when, and where you went."

"Why? Why did he do that? What did he care where I went?"

"Didn't want you a-coming back to trouble him, he didn't. I wasn't to stop you unless you circled back to the city. If you got aboard ship, or went far enough away somewheres on land, I was to come back and tell Old Adam. That's all. I'd hate to be hated like you are with that old devil, grandson though you be."

Adam felt stone cold. He stood with fists clenched, face white. "So why did you jump on me, then?"

"Jump on you? You scummy little rat. All I was a-doin' at that place was trying to have a word with you, quietlike, to tell you to get away to sea, or out West, or somewheres else out of reach of the Jervises. Then I could go home to me post in Philadelphy. A good soft berth I had there in the Jervis counting house, night-guarding it — until Old Silver Cane sent me off on your trail. You caused me to roam all over tarnation, and you cracked a bone for me. That Jenkens woman set me on a false trail down the coast to Egg Harbor. I had just had word that old Jervis had had a stroke, and Mr. Julian told me to keep track of you awhile longer. So I went into the pine barrens hunting. I was a-going home from Egg Harbor to say you had gone to sea."

He turned as if to leave, but Adam called, "Why didn't you go west looking for me?"

"That was easy, sonny, for old Garf. I prowled along Front Street and right away found a barge man mad enough to tell me a rascal of a redheaded boy had gone over the river manning a sweep for him and then run away in Jersey. I'm a tracker, I am. Don't you think I would head for ironworks when I know that's your trade?"

Shrugging his heavy shoulders as if to rid himself of all Jervises, especially the one named Quinn, Garf swung about on his heel to enter the taproom. Adam, coming to life as if recovering from a blow on the head, shouted so loudly that Job barked wildly, "Garf! You're not a constable?"

"Constable! Don't you call Garf a constable! I'd sooner see all of them kind rotting in hell than join up with 'em." He moved into the taproom.

Adam stood motionless until Job sank down and went to sleep. He reached up a hand to yank so hard on his hair that it brought water to his eyes. Then, heaving a vast sigh, Adam turned and went down the street with his ungainly dog at his heels. He turned into a driveway and along a walk made of ironstone.

In the office of the Matilda Furnace Works Hiram Joynas swiveled in his chair. "Adam, what can I do for thee?"

"Is Mr. Edwards here, sir?"

"He has but now gone into the house. Thee may find him, if thy errand be urgent, by tapping on that door."

Adam tapped. Nobody responded.

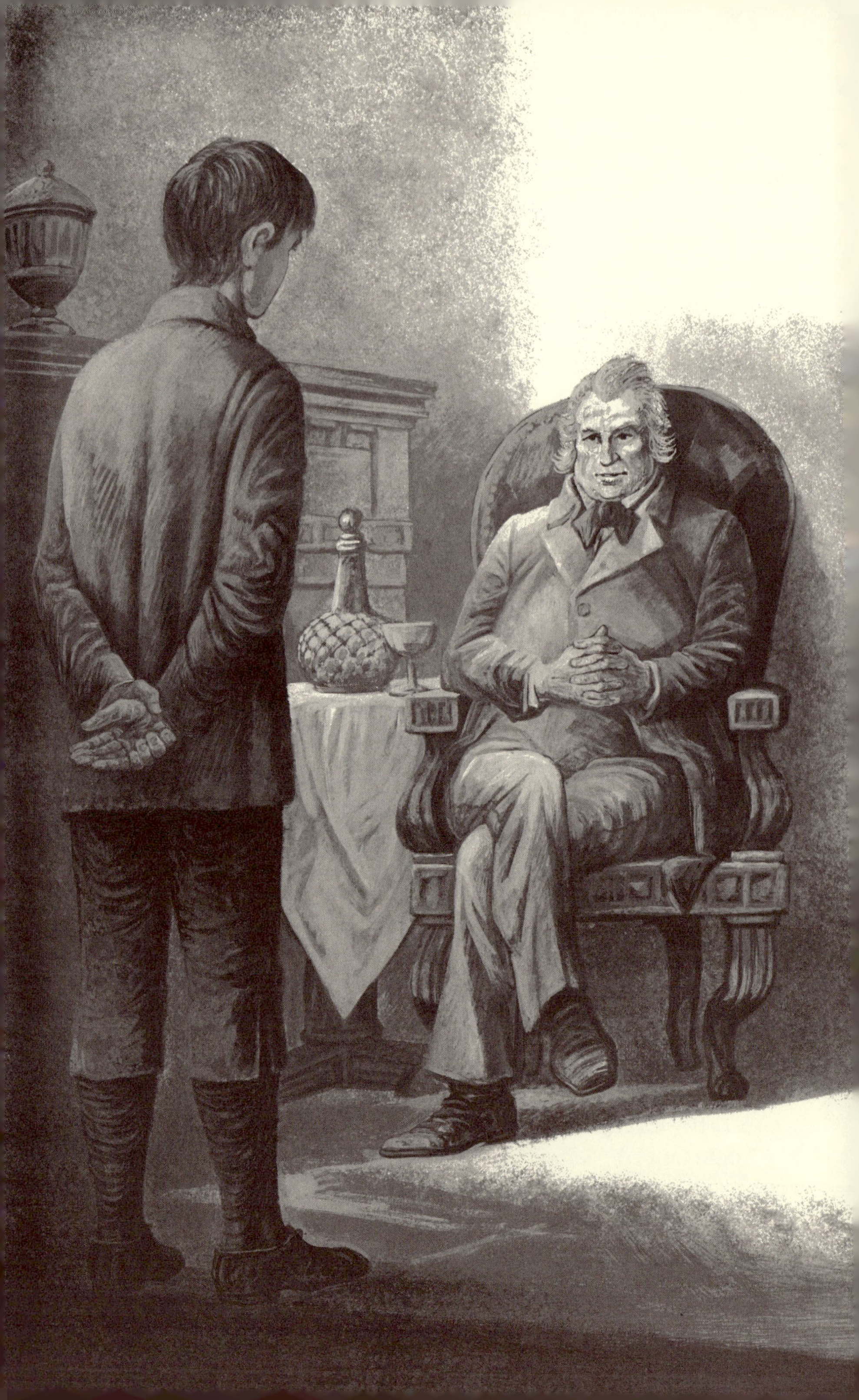

"Lad, thy touch be too timid. Give it a sound rat-tat."

Adam knocked loudly.

"Come in."

He stepped into a small parlor where a fire burned brightly in the hearth, and the ironmaster, still tired and weak from a bout with the fever, rested in a large chair with a glass of wine beside him.

"Ah, Adam Quinn. Will you take a chair and have a glass of wine?"

"I've come to turn myself in, sir. I'm a runaway bound boy."

"I suspected as much. If you wish to take the job replacing Jeff Turner I think I can arrange for your release, Adam — to be paid off by you each month out of your wages. I know a magistrate in the city who will do it for me."

"No, sir. Nobody can arrange for my release. I killed my master."

Chapter 23

Tranquility sat with hands in lap, eyes intent on Adam as he told her in as few words as possible of his unintentional killing of Bolt Sherman, and of the long running from the man he had believed to be a city constable.

"I see. So that is why thee ran so unaccountably last December. It seemed so unlike thee, Adam."

She folded and unfolded a pleat in her skirt — then she clasped her hands tightly together in her lap.

"Is the man still here?"

"No. He left by the stage. I went to the ironmaster and gave myself up."

Her face went pale, yet she said only, "Thee can count on Mr. Edwards to do all that is possible for thee with the magistrate in Philadelphia. When are they sending for thee?"

"I don't know. The ironmaster allowed me to come here to help Kip and your father. He did not ask for my word not to run away."

"He knows thee will not run again."

She got up and went to her father, who sat by the stove with head bent as if oblivious to everything around him.

"Come, Father, let me help thee to bed."

Adam went to him, "I'll help you upstairs, Mr. Willowby."

The old man raised his face. "Where's Kip?"

"He's in the barn. Come."

"Thankee, lad. Thankee."

Zack Willowby had not been the same since the death of his wife, and all of them wondered whether he would ever recover.

It was late in November and a brief thaw had set in. Adam had been at the farm nearly a week. He was helping with the fall plowing, late as it was. He stood idle for a few moments to rest his weary neck muscles and looked at the dark fringe of pines beyond the field, thinking of his wanderings in the deep barrens where few farmers and townsmen ever went. Not even ore raisers, charcoal burners, or lumbermen had penetrated this wilderness as he had. In doing so he had become a piney, for he knew and loved the barrens. Wild sounds of cedar bogs in the wind did not frighten him; the mysterious, terrifying dwarf forest could not scare him again. He felt at home with the circling hawk and the graceful little white-tailed deer leaping over treetops.

He bent to his plowing and by sundown he had finished

the field. Supper was quiet, with Tranquility pale and thin as a wisp saying little, her father eating silently, and Adam dumb with waiting. Only Kip made an attempt to talk.

"Adam," he said, "that schussel of a boy who comes by day to work here ain't worth his salt. However, tomorrow I mean to collar him. What a lie he told me about not showing up yesterday! I'll set him to digging potatoes and stand over him to see he gathers in the pumpkins. Zack, what do you say to those tactics?"

The farmer raised his head and said in a low tone, "Aye. Bring up the reinforcements." Kip, delighted at this response from the saddened old man, winked at Tranquility as if to say, "We'll get him back under that leather hat and out in the barnyard to work yet!"

His first days had been a relief to Adam — a small respite from disaster. Then relief gave way to anxiety as days passed with no word. Why did he not hear something? After his arrival his nights had provided a numbing sleep — now they became hag-ridden with fearful dreams in which the gallows stood large on its hill with a terrible burden swinging from a rope in the wind. Each morning he got up more exhausted than he had been when he went to bed. One thought haunted him. How long am I to be free? How long before they put the noose about my neck?

Watching Adam, Kip's cheerful talk dwindled. Adam took to stopping work in field or barnyard to go to the road and stare up and down it. Sometimes Kip followed him, saying, "Easy, laddie. Don't ride yourself so hard."

Adam scarcely heard him. When, at last, sound of horse and rider came he gripped the fencepost with white knuckles. Beside him Kip stiffened. A young lad drew up his mount and leaned forward. "Adam Quinn, Mr. Edwards sends word for you to wait upon him at once. At his office."

Adam nodded and Kip called out a "Thankee. Say he will be there."

They walked into the farmhouse silently. Tranquility turned from the table, hands floury, eyes questioning.

"Edwards has sent word to Adam to come at once."

"Mr. Willowby," said Adam, coming downstairs in his good clothes, "can you lend me a horse? I will see to its return this day."

"Nonsense!" shouted Kip with unnecessary force. "Give me a moment to wash up, laddie, and I'll take you in my wagon. I brought you here and I'll deliver you to Bogquake."

"God go with thee, Adam," said Tranquility.

Adam swallowed hard, unable to speak, and the ride to town was taken in a heavy silence.

They stood in the office, Kip with head cocked sideways, and Adam in a stony calm. Beside Mr. Edwards was a pudgy little old man with a vague, kind face. Adam looked around for the constable, for this man could not be a bounty hunter. The stranger seemed more like a Quaker businessman in a dark suit fitting him so tightly it looked near to bursting at the seams, and with a wide-brimmed hat on his head.

"Adam," said Mr. Edwards, "this gentleman has come in answer to my message."

"I am ready."

The man got up and came forward, hand outstretched. Adam stepped back. The stranger said, "I would not blame thee, Adam, if thee refuses my hand. Yet I hold it forth. I am thy Uncle Julian."

Adam was speechless. He could not raise his hand. Julian Jervis let his own drop to his side.

"I am come in the hope that thee will let me make some amends to my sister's son. Adam, thy grandfather is dead. For a long time I did not know what had happened to thee, after thee ran away. When going through my father's papers I saw a report of the man Garf's search, and I got in touch with him to ask him to locate thee for me. I learned of Garf's return to the city only just before Mr. Edwards' message reached me."

Adam's eyes swung to the ironmaster. So he had sent for Julian Jervis. Had he also sent word to the authorities?

"Adam, will thee listen to me with patience for a little — I — ?"

All the bitterness and pain of his life rose in Adam's throat and burst forth in a flood. "What use is there in asking me for patience? What good is your talk — your fine, smooth Jervis talk? What is talk to a man wanted by the authorities? Who will take the word of a runaway bound boy who is accused of killing his master?"

The portly Quaker took a quick step forward. "Killing thy master? Does thee not know that Bolt Sherman is alive and, save for a limp, as whole and strong as ever?"

Adam swayed sideways and then jerked himself upright before Kip could reach out to support him. Kip grabbed his shoulders, nevertheless, and sat him down in a chair.

"A good idea," said Mr. Edwards. "Sit down yourself, Mr. Kip. And Mr. Jervis."

"Not dead? Bolt Sherman is not dead — I thought —"

"Not dead he, Adam. Indeed, never did I see a scoundrel more alive. Now listen to me, nephew. I could not hold my father in check, nor did I have the courage ever to try.

Call me a spineless dolt if thee wishes. I was not born with hardness, and it took more hardness than anyone on earth could possess to stand up to Old Adam. Yet I never liked nor wanted him to treat thee so. I did protest, for what it was worth, which was nothing at all. I grieved for my sister, too.

"When my father died the first thing I did was seek out Bolt Sherman, who had posted bills for your apprehension as a runaway bound boy, and pay him all and more for thy release — and more than enough to keep him from bringing thee to the law for assault. His sly journeyman did tell me something, demanding a sum of money for the information. I gave it him. He admitted he saw thee push past thy master at the stair head, and he saw thy master trip and fall. He knows there was no attack other than that. And Bolt Sherman knows he knows it."

Mr. Jervis leaned forward, hands on knees. "And now, Adam, thee is free. Can thee understand that? Free."

Kip was laughing, slapping his leg, giving out with some hallooing shouts of joy, and Mr. Edwards began to chuckle. Hiram Joynas, who had left the room at the entrance of the visitor, thrust his head in and showed such an amazed face that the ironmaster had to wave him away.

"All right, Hiram. Jubilation. That's all. Mr. Kip is not having a raging fit."

Adam didn't laugh. He was numb. Then, as he began to take it in, as the word *free* hit him, he heaved a sigh of such proportions that it sent Kip off to laughing again. Adam set his jaw and said, "I want to know how my father died."

In the silence his uncle flushed. "I thought thee had been told. Patrick Quinn was slain by an outlaw named

Murrell on the Natchez Trace in the western wilderness. I believe thy father was on his way to Philadelphia. So it was indicated by a man who was with him on the journey, and who escaped and wrote to thy grandfather. That letter I found in his desk, along with a report from Garf, and with a packet of letters addressed to you, sent in care of 'The Honorable Adam Jervis, Esquire.'" Julian Jervis' troubled face turned grim. "My father was hard, but I had not known before how cruel."

Adam's shoulders sagged. He drew in a long breath, and as the words sank deeply into his mind his head came up, eyes wide with a sudden light. His father had written to him. He had been returning for him. He had not forgotten.

"The letters?"

"I will place them in thy hand as soon as thee returns to the city. And, Adam — I have some plans. Thee is to become a full-fledged member of the firm, with a share and a name the equal of my son Thomas."

Adam dropped his eyes to his hands, where black earth rimmed the nails, where iron dust had been ground into the skin until metal had become a part of his body. His mind was working now. How clearly it was working! A silence fell as they waited.

"I thankee, Uncle Julian. I hold nothing against you. Yet I cannot accept your offer. I do not want to be in a mercantile house."

"Then what does thee want?"

Adam suddenly felt as if he had known what he wanted all of his life.

"I want to be a doctor. I don't know how. I know that is all I want to be."

Julian opened his eyes wide in surprise, then he made a slow inclination of his head. "Well, Adam, will thee let me help thee to that?"

Kip broke in, soberly this time. "Adam, I have a brother who thinks nothing of my work, my life, or my choice of clothing. He tells me so each time we meet. Yet he will take my word for it that you will make the best physician's apprentice he has ever had. And — although I hate to say so of anyone so pious a Quaker, and so lacking in adventurous spirit — Dr. Charles Lafitte is the man for you."

Julian nodded slow agreement. "Yes, he is right, although I do not see how Dr. Lafitte could have a brother of your name and appearance — I beg thy pardon, sir, but astonishment took me over completely." Julian's face was apple red.

Kip grinned, green eyes wrinkling with amusement. "You are not the first to say it and will not be the last, it kreissels me to admit." Kip then hooted with laughter. "It takes all kinds, even in the same family, as you Jervises should know."

"And now, Adam," said Julian, "I do understand thy feelings. I know thee does not want the help of a family that has treated thee so badly. Yet I will take it as a kindness if thee will let me pay thy way in thy schooling."

Adam turned to Kip. "You mean Dr. Lafitte will take me as a medical apprentice?"

"He cannot refuse you, me laddie. For if he should be so foolish I will change his mind by hook or by crook. I will resort to blackmail, if necessary, and threaten to put into the newsprint an account of how a certain young chap broke Hanover Friends Meeting House windows with a judicious aiming of his catapult and a few rocks — in which art Charles was a master in his youth. This will solve a mystery of long standing in our childhood town, and will ruin my Quaker brother's unblemished reputation. Never fear, he will take you."

"I know of Dr. Lafitte's reputation," said the ironmaster with a twinkle in his eye. "He can fit you well for the Medical School, and for the University at Edinburgh in Scotland — if you have a mind for that much scholarly effort."

In a long silence Adam said, "All right, Kip. I'll be a bound boy again, and this time of my own free will."

"Good!" Glancing at Julian Jervis, Kip said, "Adam, your uncle will feel better for the rest of his life if you will not be a stubborn, pride-puffed Irishman and will accept his offer to pay your way."

Another pause fell on them — then Adam said, "I will accept your offer to pay for my apprenticeship, Uncle Julian. And be grateful for it."

The ironmaster heaved himself to his feet and brought in a decanter of his best port wine to drink to the future of Adam Quinn.

As they left together, Adam said with a wry grin, "So here I am, Kip, right back where I started — older but not much wiser — and a bound boy. With Jervis money, too."

"Bound you will be and for some years, Adam. But a boy you are not anymore."

Chapter 24

"I'LL GO OUT and put the old mare into harness," said Kip, "then we'll be on our way. No — don't come along. I don't need help, for I could do it in me sleep, if need be, and never miss a buckle."

Adam rose from the Willowbys' table and went upstairs, to come down presently with his father's knapsack. Tranquility was scouring kettles with sand and ashes. Job was spread out before the stove like a rumpled rug. At one side Mr. Willowby sat silently in his chair. With a sudden flush, Adam surprised himself by saying, "I want to talk to you alone, Quillie."

She looked at him, put down her kettle, washed off her hands and went with him into the chilly parlor. They stood facing each other. Adam shifted his weight from one foot to the other, hands clenching and unclenching, only to yank on his forelock. He had just noticed that around her neck, on the demure gray gown, she was wearing a thin gold chain with a cameo locket. Tranquility burst into a giggle such as Adam had not heard since those teaching evenings at the Hobson home.

"Has thee lost thy tongue, Adam? Did thee ask me in here to stare while thee joggles from one foot to the other and tries to pull thy hair out by the roots?"

He gave way to a sheepish grin, letting his fingers loose, trying to stand solid-footed.

"You have not said when you are leaving for Indian country. I — well — I want to know before I go. When?"

Her voice sobered, eyes sad. "I have sent word to Philadelphia Meeting that I am not going with the mission. Did thee think I would leave my father alone?"

"I'm glad you aren't going."

"'Tis thee who goes and is not returning," she said. "Thee will be a solemn, portly physician someday in fine linen and black broadcloth. Thee will say, 'Ah, my good lady,' or perhaps, 'my good sir,' as the case may be. 'Ah, let me inform thee of the latest scientific information in the medical profession — and do not contradict me, madam or sir, for I know so much that thee, with thy lack of higher education can never understand. Hummm! Yes.'"

"Now, Quillie," said Adam, "don't you fault me. How can a bound-out boy ever get like that?"

"Bound boys have done so before this. And like all the others, thee will come into the room with the apothecary or barber, to bleed folks and purge them with calomel."

"No, I will not!" Adam's voice rang out so loudly that Kip, entering by the front, thrust his head into the door of the parlor. "No, that I will not do. I mean to learn all I can be taught, both as apprentice to the doctor and in the Medical School. Then, perhaps I'll go to Edinburgh for some more study. Yet will I never bleed anyone, nor make the teeth drop out."

"Well, laddie," called out Kip, "that I rejoice to hear, although I can tell you this — you will find it hard to get through your schooling and not do so. Charles does as little bleeding as he possibly can, never lets out much, even by applying leeches — but he is roundly trounced by other medical men for it — in words, and in writings — and often, too. Prosperous mercantile burghers demand that their medical men withdraw their life force in quantity."

"That matters no whit to me," said Adam. "I do not mean to practice medicine in that city, or any city. I am going to return to the pines, where I intend to spend my life henceforth and forever. This I have already told Dr. Micah in a message I sent to Crossroads House."

"Good — good indeed — and what's more, I think you will," said Kip.

Zack Willoughby came slowly into the parlor and stood looking at the portrait of his wife. The others fell silent as he said in a voice scarcely heard, "She had the prettiest little feet in the world."

Kip broke into a stricken silence. "Come, lad, the sun grows warm, day advances, and if I am to transport you to the City of Brotherly Love we must be off. Zack, we will bid you farewell, but only for a time."

"Mr. Kip," said Willowby, turning around, "I cannot

thank you enough, nor Adam Quinn neither, and so I will not try."

"If you want to thank me, sir, just gather in your friends and line them up to have their portraits painted come next spring — painted by the best wandering limner ever came rolling through these parts. Next season will be my last with the wagon, for I am almost ready to retire Hendrickje to pasture and board ship for the Netherlands. A goodly sum in my money pouch next season will get me off in fine fettle."

"If that thee wishes, that thee shall have," said the farmer in his old, emphatic way. "I will order out the cavalry, marshall the foot soldiers, get the artillery on the road, and go into battle with flags flying. Thee shall have enough Friends to limn to keep thee right here through the heat of summer."

They looked at each other, delighted to see the old Zack rising in him.

"I thank thee, Adam," said Tranquility, as she impulsively and with no regard for Quaker decorum, thrust out her hands. Taking courage in both hands, as it were, he enclosed hers in his big ones. Said she, looking down, "Thy hands are more fit for a drover than a learned doctor's. Yet I think they will do what thee asks of them. If thee needs more teaching than can be gotten in the great cities, then come back to the Meeting House school, Adam. Thee will find me there, ready to learn thee thy letters."

Her voice laughed at him, yet her face was as pink as if she wore the rosy-lined Quaker bonnet lying above the stairs in a clothespress. By way of reply, Adam turned red and dropped her hands. Kip grinned, clucked in mock disapproval, and said, "As for Adam, he does not say what favor you can do for him, farmer Willowby, by way of a thankee. Yet I think you will discover it in time. I'll be kreisseled if I don't believe you will."

"Tranquility," shouted Adam, leaning out of the wagon over Job's shaggy head, to get a last glimpse of her in the doorway, "I'll be back sometimes — if I have to come on shank's mare. As Dr. Micah would say, 'It's only a whoop and a holler to here.'"